Japanese Monograph No. 76

AIR OPERATIONS IN THE CHINA AREA

July 1937 – August 1945

PREPARED BY
HEADQUARTERS, USAFFE
AND EIGHTH U.S. ARMY (REAR)

DISTRIBUTED BY
OFFICE OF THE CHIEF OF MILITARY HISTORY
DEPARTMENT OF THE ARMY

Published by Books Express Publishing
Copyright © Books Express, 2012
ISBN 978-1-78039-839-6

Books Express publications are available from all good retail and online booksellers. For publishing proposals and direct ordering please contact us at: info@books-express.com

PREFACE

This monograph is one of a series prepared under instructions from the Supreme Commander for the Allied Powers to the Japanese Government (SCAPIN No. 126, 12 Oct 1945). The series covers not only the operations of the Japanese armed forces during World War II but also their operations in China and Manchuria which preceded the world conflict. The original studies were written by former officers of the Japanese Army and Navy under the supervision of the Historical Records Section of the First (Army) and Second (Navy) Demobilization Bureaus of the Japanese Government. The manuscripts were translated by the Military Intelligence Service Group, G2, Headquarters, Far East Command. Extensive editing was accomplished by the Japanese Research Division of the Office of the Military History Officer, Headquarters, United States Army Forces, Far East and Eighth United States Army (Rear).

The writers were handicapped in the preparation of the basic manuscript by the non-availability of many operational records which are normally employed as source material in this type of study. Many official orders, plans and unit journals were lost during operations or were destroyed at the cessation of hostilities. A particular handicap has been the lack of strength reports. Most of the important orders and other information sources, however, have been reconstructed from memory and while not textually identical with the originals are believed to be accurate and reliable.

As the name indicates, this monograph recounts the planning and conduct of the air operations in the China theater from the outbreak of the China Incident in July 1937 to the cessation of hostilities in August 1945.

The basic manuscript was written by Major Takejiro Shiba, an Imperial General Headquarters staff officer. It was based on documents in the possession of Colonel Genichi Yamamoto, Air Group Staff Officer; Colonel Hiroshi Sasao, 3d Air Group Staff Officer; Lt Colonel Hirokichi Mizuo and Major En Komatsu, Fifth Air Army Staff Officers; and Major Takejiro Shiba as well as on information supplied from memory by these officers. Subsequent research by the Japanese Research Division revealed a number of inaccuracies in the original manuscript and large portions have been rewritten to effect the necessary corrections. In addition, pertinent information has been inserted where it was felt necessary for clarity or that it would add interest to the document.

The History Section, Army War College, Japanese Self-Defense Force, which has been collecting documents on the China Incident, has proved most helpful in placing its sources at the disposal of the Japanese Research Division.

The editor has received valuable assistance in research and in the preparation of maps and charts from Tadao Shudo, formerly a lieutenant colonel on the staff of the Eleventh Army in central China and later a member of the Army General Staff and Air Army General Staff.

All maps submitted with this monograph were drawn by the Japanese Research Division and the spelling of place names in the text and on the maps is that used in AMS 5301.

Other monographs covering the operations of the Japanese armed forces in the China area are:

Mono No	Title	Period
70*	China Area Operations Record	Jul 37 - Nov 41
71*	Army Operations in China	Dec 41 - Dec 43
72*	Army Operations in China	Jan 44 - Aug 45
74*	Operations in the Kun-lun-kuan Area	Dec 39 - Feb 40
129*	China Area Operations Record: Command of China Expeditionary Army	Aug 43 - Aug 45
130*	China Area Operations Record: Sixth Area Army Operations	May 44 - Aug 45
166	China Incident Naval Air Operations	Jul 37 - Nov 37
178*	North China Area Operations Record	Jul 37 - May 41
179*	Central China Area Operations Record	1937 - 1941
180*	South China Area Operations Record	1937 - 1941

* Indicates edit completed.

Tokyo, Japan
10 December 1956

Table of Contents

	Page
CHAPTER 1 - Air Operations in China, 1937	15
Outline of Air Operations in North China	19
Outline of Air Operations in Central and South China	27
CHAPTER 2 - Air Operations in China, 1938	35
Air Operations Prior to the Tungshan Operation	35
Air Operations in North China	38
Air Operations in Central China	41
Air Operations During the Battle of Tungshan	44
Air Operations During the Wu-Han Operation	48
Reorganization and Order of Battle of Air Group	48
Preparations for Wu-Han Operation	49
Summary of Air Operations During the Wu-Han Operation	53
Air Operations Over North China to Support the Wu-Han Operation	57
Air Operations After the Occupation of Wu-Han	59
CHAPTER 3 - Operations in China, 1939	69
Outline of First Air Operation (24 Dec 38 - 28 Feb 39)	69
Outline of Air Operation in Szechwan Province	71

	Page
Outline of Air Operation in Lanchow Area	72
Outline of Second Air Operation (1 Oct 1939 - 31 Oct 1939)	73
Progress of Operations	81
Outline of Third Air Operation (10 Dec 1939 - 31 Dec 1939)	82
Summary of Naval Air Operations	83
Summary of Other Operations	83

CHAPTER 4 - Air Operations in China, 1940 85

    Summary of Tactical Command of Air Operations in the Spring of 1940 85

        General Situation and Disposition of 3d Air Group 85

    Air Operations During the Ichang Operation 87

    Direction of Air Operations in China by Imperial General Headquarters 88

    Outline of Fourth Air Operation (29 Apr 1940 - 10 Sep 1940) 91

    Outline of Air Operations During the Occupation of French Indo-China 93

CHAPTER 5 - Air Operations in China, 1941 95

    Outline of Air Operations During the Eastern Chekiang Operation 95

    Outline of Air Operations During the Chungyuan Operation 96

    Outline of Fifth Air Operation 97

	Page
CHAPTER 6 - Pacific War (Dec 1941 - Dec 1942)	103
Outline of Air Operations During the Hong Kong Operation	103
Outline of Operational Progress	104
Outline of Air Operations During the 2d Changsha Operation	106
Outline of Air Operations During the Chekiang-Kiangsi Operation	107
Return of 3d Air Division to China	111
Disposition of Air Forces under the Command of the 3d Air Division and Progress of Operations	111
Tactical Command of Imperial General Headquarters	113
CHAPTER 7 - Air Operations in China, 1943	117
Direction by Imperial General Headquarters in 1943	117
Progress of Air Operations in China	119
Southern Army's Air Operations Against China	128
Navy Air Operations	128
Preparations for Air Operations During the Summer	128
3d Air Division's Summer Air Operations Plan	129
Progress of Operation	131
First Phase (23 Jul to 22 Aug)	131
Second Phase (22 Aug to 8 Sep)	132
Third Phase (9 Sep to 7 Oct)	134

	Page
Air Operations from October to December	137
CHAPTER 8 - Army Air Operations in China, 1944	143
General Situation	143
Fifth Air Army's Plan	145
Estimate of Enemy Air Force Activities	145
Situation Prior to the Operation (mid-Feb to mid-Apr 1944)	148
Peiping-Hankou Operation (mid-Apr - end May 1944)	149
Hunan-Kwangsi Operation (end May 1944 - Jan 1945)	151
To the Fall of Hengyang	151
Outline of Air Operation	159
Enemy Air Force Situation	162
Enemy Attacks and Tactics	164
From the Fall of Hengyang to the End of Ichi-Go Operation	165
General Situation of Ground Operations	165
Fifth Air Army Situation	168
Tactical Command	173
Outline of Operations by Fifth Air Army Units	177
Enemy Air Force Situation	178
Estimates on B-29's	180
Intelligence Network to Cope with B-29's	181

		Page
	Interception	182
	Air Raids Over Bases in Chengtu	183
CHAPTER 9 -	Preparations for Operations Along the China Coast, Jan - Aug 1945	185
	Japanese Air Force Situation	185
	Enemy Air Force Situation	186
	Direction of Operations and Tactics	187
	Attacks from the Sea	190
	Fifth Air Army's Preparations Against Attacks from the Sea	190
	Organization of the 13th Air Division	191
	Preparations for Air Operations in Central and North China	193
	Main Points of the Operational Plan to Protect the China Coast	194
	Battle Plan of 13th Air Division in the Event of an Enemy Attack in the Vicinity of Shanghai	195
	Situation at Termination of Hostilities	202
	Escort of Transport Convoys	207
	Air Operations During the Okinawa Campaign	208
	Operations Against the Russian Army	211

CHARTS

No. 1	Japanese Army Planes Used in China in 1937	18
No. 2	The Navy Airplanes Used During China Incident, 1937	29

		Page
No. 3	Outline of Order of Battle of the Air Group in China, 6 Aug 1938	50
No. 4	Distribution of Army and Navy Air Strength, 2 Dec 1938	64
No. 5	Disposition of Air Force in China, Sep 1939	79
No. 6	Disposition of 3d Air Group, Mar 1940	86
No. 7	Fifth Air Army's Strength and Disposition, May 1944	154
No. 8	Actual Status of Pilots of the Fifth Air Army as of 31 May 1944	156
No. 9	Estimated Disposition of the Enemy Air Strength in China (May 1944 to Dec 1944)	163
No. 10	Enemy Attacks, May 1944 - Oct 1944	166
No. 11	Disposition and Mission of the Fifth Air Army (From the time of the attack on Hengyang to the Occupation of Liuchowhsien)	170
No. 12	Number and Skill of Pilots of the Fifth Air Army, reported end Aug 1944	174
No. 13	Estimated Disposition of Enemy Front-line Planes in China, 20 Jul 1945	188
No. 14	Special Attack Units, Aug 1945	196

MAPS

No. 1	General Reference Map - Chapter 1	14
No. 2	General Reference Map - Chapter 2	34
No. 3	General Reference Map - Chapters 3, 4, 5	68
No. 4	Disposition of the 3d Air Group, Aug 1941	99

		Page
No. 5	General Reference Map - Chapter 6	102
No. 6	General Reference Map - Chapter 7	116
No. 7	General Reference Map - Chapters 8, 9	142
No. 8	13th Division's Battle Plan (Shanghai Area), Jul 1945	200
No. 9	Operational Area for Convoy Escort, Jan - Feb 1945	205
Index		213

GENERAL REFERENCE MAP – CHAPTER
MAP NO. 1

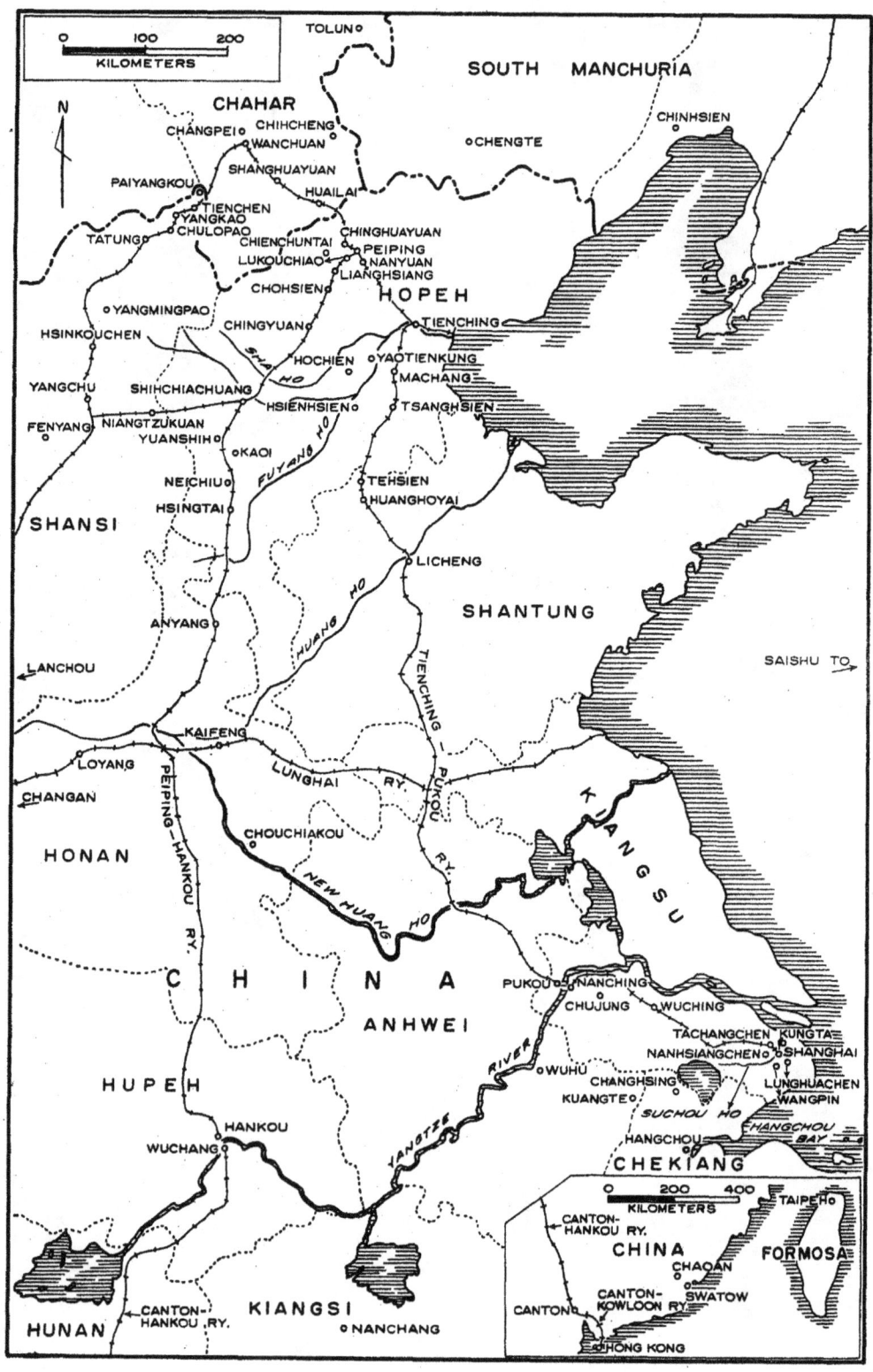

CHAPTER 1

Air Operations in China

1937

After the outbreak of the China Incident on 7 July 1937, in order to support its army should negotiations fail, on 11 July the Army and Navy General Staffs of the Central Authorities[1] published the following agreement in regard to air operations:

> Should the need arise, the Army will assume responsibility for destroying the enemy air force in north China while the Navy will be responsible for destroying the enemy air force in central and south China.

During the first year of the China Incident the Army and Navy air forces carried out air operations in accordance with this agreement.

Immediately after the outbreak of the Incident, the Provisional Air Group was dispatched from Japan to Tienching via south Manchuria. The organization of the Group was:

Provisional Air Group Commander: Lt Gen Baron Yoshitoshi Tokugawa

Provisional Air Group Headquarters

1st Air Brigade Headquarters

---

1. Prior to 17 November 1937, when Imperial General Headquarters was established in Tokyo to cope with the situation in China, Central Authorities comprised the Army and Navy General Staffs and the War and Navy Ministries.

1st Air Battalion (2 squadrons - reconnaissance)

2d Air Battalion (2 squadrons - reconnaissance)

3d Air Battalion (2 squadrons - fighter)

5th Air Battalion (2 squadrons - light bomber)

6th Air Battalion (2 squadrons - heavy bomber)

8th Air Battalion (2 squadrons - fighter)

9th Air Battalion (2 squadrons - light bomber)

3d Independent Air Squadron (heavy bomber)

4th Independent Air Squadron (reconnaissance)

6th Independent Air Squadron (reconnaissance)

9th Independent Air Squadron (fighter)

On its arrival in south Manchuria on 26 July the Provisional Air Group was placed under the command of the commander of the North China Garrison Army when the following directive was issued by the Central Authorities:

> The use of planes will be restricted, as far as possible, to close cooperation with land operations.
>
> International relations will be taken into consideration when targets are being chosen for ground strafing and bombing.

The Air Group, therefore, adopted a policy of attacking such objectives as threatened the Japanese sphere of influence rather than aggressively attacking enemy air planes to destroy them.

Prior to the China Incident, because the Army's policy had been to train its air units to support ground operations, even the heavy bombers had a striking range of only 450 km,[2] whereas the Navy planes, which were trained to carry out long-distance bombings over the water, had a striking range of about 1,500 km. In addition, in order to replenish its short supply of bombers, the Army had equipped reconnaissance and fighter planes with bomb release mechanism but, because of their limited load capacity, the type of bombs carried was small and the reconstructed planes were not very effective.

The type and number of planes planned for use in the China theater at the outbreak of the Incident were:[3]

	Army	Navy
Reconnaissance planes	82	21
Fighters	100	69
Light bombers	24	54
Heavy bombers	24	50
Torpedo planes	-	27
Total	230	221

---

2. See Chart No. 1.

3. These figures do not include the Kwantung Army planes used in the Chahar area. The Navy planes included carrier planes, seaplanes and land planes but in this table Army nomenclature has been used.

Chart No. 1

Japanese Army Planes Used in China in 1937

Types	Model	Max Speed (kph)	Ceiling (m)	Range (km)	Armament		Model Year
					Guns (No x mm)	Bombs (No x kg)	
Heavy Bomber	93A	235	5,000	900	3 x 7.7	1,000 kg	1932
Light Bomber	93A	263	7,000	900	2 x 7.7	300 - 400 kg	1932
Reconnaissance	94	300		800	3 x 7.7		1934
Fighter	95B	394	10,000	800	2 x 7.7		1936
Fighter	97	470	12,250	825 - 1,710	2 x 7.7		1937

Outline of Air Operations in North China

On 7 July, as soon as news of the Lukouchiao Incident was received, the Kwantung Army commander dispatched part of the air force under his command to the vicinity of the North China - Manchurian border. On the 11th, the unit, known as the Composite Air Brigade and composed of the 12th Air Battalion (2 squadrons - heavy bombers) the 15th Air Battalion (2 squadrons - reconnaissance) and the 16th Air Battalion (2 squadrons - fighters), was placed under the command of the North China Garrison Army commander.

On its arrival in south Manchuria on 26 July, the Provisional Air Group, in accordance with an Army order, assumed command of the Composite Air Brigade. The Brigade then became known as the Provisional Air Brigade. The following day the Group's main force advanced to the Tienching airfield and from there supported ground operations in the Peiping-Tienching sector. Its bombing of Nanyuan and Chinghuayuan contributed greatly to the success of the ground attacks on these cities.[4]

On 16 August, in order to destroy Wanchuan, which was the headquarters of the Chinese 143d Division, the Kwantung Army dispatched

---

4. Ground operations of the North China Garrison Army are described in detail in Monograph No. 178, North China Area Operations Record, July 1937 - May 1941.

the 2d Air Group[5] (commanded by Maj Gen Saburo Ando) to Chinhsien. Using Chengte, Tolun and Changpei airfields, as advanced bases, this Air Group bombed Wanchuan and inflicted heavy casualties on the enemy. At the same time, the Air Group cooperated with the attack of the 2d Mixed Brigade (Kwantung Army) by destroying enemy positions in the vicinity of Wanchuan.

After having successfully attacked Tatung and harassed the enemy in that area, the Air Group, in compliance with a Kwantung Army order, assigned the Provisional Air Brigade (six squadrons commanded by Col Kamijo) to support the Chahar Operation. The main force returned to its home base in Manchuria during the latter part of August.

During the Chahar Operation (mid-August - mid-October 1937) an element of the Provisional Air Group, using the Chengte airfield, greatly assisted the 11th Independent Mixed Brigade and the 5th Division by bombing enemy positions along the border of Hopeh-Chahar Provinces. It also supplied ammunition and rations to the Sakata Detachment (an element of the 11th Independent Mixed Brigade) when this Detachment was surrounded by the enemy. Subsequently, with the advance of the North China Garrison Army, the Air Group searched

---

5. The 2d Air Group was composed of the 10th Air Battalion (2 squadrons - reconnaissance and 2 squadrons - light bombers), the 11th Air Battalion (2 squadrons - fighters) 12th Air Battalion (4 squadrons - heavy bombers) 15th Air Battalion (2 squadrons - reconnaissance) and 16th Air Battalion (2 squadrons - fighters and 2 squadrons - light bombers).

out and inflicted heavy damage on the enemy withdrawing to the Huailai Plain and to the west thereof. Later, a part of the reconnaissance unit supported the 5th Division from Nanyuan air base and the advance airfield at Wanchuan.

On 20 August, an agreement was reached between the North China Garrison Army and the Kwantung Army in regard to air operations. This agreement stated:

> The North China Garrison Army unit at Chengte will transfer immediately to the Nanyuan airfield and the Kwantung Army air unit will use either the Chengte or Tolun airfield.
>
> The boundary line between the two armies will temporarily be a line connecting Chihcheng, Shanghuayuan, Paiyangkou (10 km north of Tienchen) and the Outer Great Wall. The North China Garrison Army will be responsible for the area along the line. However, should the occasion demand, the Kwantung Army will carry out attacks in the vicinity of Tatung.

During the first half of September, the Provisional Air Brigade greatly assisted the operation of the Chahar Expeditionary Group of the Kwantung Army by cooperating in attacks against strong enemy positions in the vicinity of Tienchen, Chulopao and Tatung by conducting reconnaissance and bombing raids from Wanchuan. As soon as the Japanese first-line troops captured Yangkao on 8 September, the Provisional Air Brigade advanced its base to this town.

Just after the Lukouchiao Incident, enemy planes were sighted in the vicinity of the Lunghai railway, but with the opening of hostilities in Shanghai on 9 August, these planes were transferred to the Shanghai area. During the early days of the China Incident no planes were sighted in north China. However, in mid-September, the enemy established an air base in the vicinity of Yangchu and, from there, counterattacked the Japanese forces in Chahar Province.[6] The Provisional Air Brigade immediately attacked Yangchu from its base at Yangkao and, for the first time, engaged the enemy in air combat in north China. Seventeen enemy planes were shot down.

During the latter part of September, in accordance with Army orders, the Provisional Air Brigade returned to its home base in Manchuria. It was replaced at Yangkao by the Provisional Air Unit (10th Air Battalion, composed of two squadrons). Until mid-December, the Provisional Air Unit cooperated mainly with the operation of the Chahar Expeditionary Group of the Kwantung Army.

Previously, in mid-August, the Provisional Air Group had advanced its main force to the Nanyuan airfield and supported the 20th Division in its attack against and capture of the northwest plateau of Lianghsiang. In the beginning of September, by completely destroying the enemy positions, it assisted in the progress of the attack of the Ushijima Detachment against a superior enemy force in the vicinity of Chienchuntai. About 10 September, part of the Pro-

---

6. In the early stages of the Incident the Chinese Air Force was equipped with British Gloucester "Gladiator" single-seat multigun fighters, Russian I-15 single-seat biplanes and I-16 single-seat fighter monoplanes, and United States Curtiss "Hawk" single-seat biplane fighters.

visional Air Group supported the 10th Division's attack against Ma-chang.

On 31 August 1937, the order of battle of the North China Area Army was published and the Provisional Air Group was placed under the direct command of the Area Army commander.[7] The Air Group was then ordered to reconnoiter enemy positions from air bases at Nan-yuan and Tienching for the Area Army and the First and Second Armies. Further, the Air Group, having carried out reconnaissance of the flooded area in Hopeh Province, was able to furnish valuable data for the North China Area Army's operational plan.

Immediately after the outbreak of fighting in Shanghai,[8] the Provisional Air Group transferred one air squadron to the Shanghai Expeditionary Army. In mid-September, the Air Group was reinforced by the addition of the headquarters of the 4th Air Brigade and two air squadrons. The Air Group was then composed of the 1st Air Brigade, the 4th Air Brigade and an air unit directly attached to the commander. The 1st Air Brigade supported the operations of the First Army and the 4th Air Brigade those of the Second Army. The air unit directly attached to the commander was used for long distance reconnaissance and to assist the two air brigades.

---

7. Ground operations of the North China Area Army are described in detail in Monograph No. 178, North China Area Operations Record July 1937 - May 1941.

8. Monograph No. 179, Central China Area Operations Record, 1937 - 1941.

During the Chohsien-Chingyuan Operation in September, not only did the 1st Air Brigade give the First Army direct air cover to facilitate its operations but, by bombing such towns as Chingyuan and Shihchiachuang, it assisted the First Army's advance and lowered the enemy's morale. In addition, by promptly reporting enemy positions, the 1st Air Brigade helped to accelerate preparations for the First Army's pursuit action.

As the Second Army was experiencing great difficulty in regard to lines of communication, the 4th Air Brigade liaisoned between the groups and simplified the direction of the Army's operation. During the attack on Tsanghsien, the Air Brigade not only bombed enemy positions in and around the town but also bombed such key points behind the enemy lines as Yaotienkung, Hsienhsien and Hochien in order to sever the enemy's retreat routes.

During the operations in the vicinity of Shihchiachuang and the Fuyang Ho in the early part of October, the Air Group advanced its main force to airfields to the south and north of Chingyuan. The 1st Air Brigade cooperated with the First Army while the 4th Air Brigade cooperated with the Second Army. At this time, the heavy bomber units of both air brigades were placed under the direct command of the Provisional Air Group. These heavy bomber units cooperated with the pursuit action carried out by the ground forces by bombing the railway bridge across the Sha Ho, Hsingtai and Anyang stations, and Yuanshih, Neichiu and Kaoi in order to check the enemy's withdrawal.

An attack was launched against Yangchu in early October. The Air Group advanced its main force to the Yangkao and Shihchiachuang airfields and participated in this operation. At the same time, part of the units under the direct command of the Provisional Air Group cooperated with the Second Army from the Tienching airfield.

When the 5th Division attacked and captured Hsinkouchen on 13 October, part of the 1st Air Brigade from Yangkao and later from Yangmingpao cooperated with the Division while the main body of the Air Brigade cooperated with the 20th Division by bombing Niangtzukuan from Shihchiachuang. This generally assisted in the favorable development of the battle in this area.

From early November the Yangchu Operation developed favorably and the Air Group continued to cooperate with the ground units in the pursuit action by repeatedly attacking the withdrawing enemy units. Later, the Air Group facilitated the attack on Yangchu castle by bombing the vicinity of the north gate of the castle.

Although at the end of September enemy planes near Yangchu were completely wiped out by the Provisional Air Brigade of the Kwantung Army, the enemy air force later recovered its strength and frequently attacked the Japanese 5th Division and the area along the Peiping-Hankou railway. In late October, the Air Group bombed Fenyang airfield and destroyed two enemy planes. At the same time, one enemy plane was shot down at Yangchu and eight planes were destroyed on the ground. In early November the Air Group repeatedly attacked Yangchu and prevented enemy planes from operating in the area.

After the Yangchu Operation, the Air Group received reinforcements of new heavy bombers (Type 97 - heavy bombers with a striking range of about 800 km). On 11 November, the Air Group used these reinforcements to carry out a surprise attack against Loyang airfield. Several enemy planes were damaged on the ground and one plane was shot down. On the 12th, the Air Group carried out a surprise attack against Changan and destroyed an unknown number of planes on the ground.

As the result of an agreement between the Air Group and the 1st Combined Navy Air Force, on 17 November, the Navy was assigned the mission of bombing Lunghai railway, Changan, Loyang and Chouchiakou (approximately 150 km south of Kaifeng). The Air Group then ceased its attacks on the Lunghai railway and in the southern area.

On 19 November, the 1st Combined Navy Air Force (17 land attack planes - heavy bombers with a 1500 km striking range) began attacks from the Nanyuan airfield against enemy air bases at Loyang, Changan, Chouchiakou and Lanchow. Although details are not available, the results of these attacks were regarded as most successful.

In early December, the 4th Air Brigade Headquarters and eight air squadrons of the Provisional Air Group were transferred to central China and to other areas. Part of the Air Group was stationed in the Peiping-Hankou railway sector and at Yangchu while its main force used Tehsien and Huanghoyai airfields as their bases in order to support the Second Army's operation to occupy Licheng. This operation was to be undertaken about the end of December.

During the Huang Ho Crossing Operation, the Air Group proved extremely helpful in reconnoitering enemy positions and the terrain. After the crossing, the Group's main force attacked the withdrawing enemy and inflicted heavy losses on them.

Outline of Air Operations in Central and South China

In accordance with the Army-Navy Agreement, the Navy was responsible for destroying the enemy air strength in central China.

With the landing of the Shanghai Expeditionary Army at the mouth of the Huangpu River on 23 August 1937[11] the Navy Air Force attacked enemy bases at Shanghai, Nanchang, Hangchou, Nanching and Chujung from carriers and air bases in Formosa and Saishu To. This force destroyed the greater part of the advance units of the Chinese Air Force and secured air supremacy in the Shanghai area.

The Navy Air Force cooperated closely with the Shanghai Expeditionary Army during landing operations and later in attacks on

---

11. Monograph No. 179, <u>Central China Area Operations Record, 1937 - 1941</u>.

Chinese forces in the vicinity of Shanghai.

The types and number of Navy planes used during the early stage of the China Incident are shown on Chart No. 2.

In the early part of September, an Army reconnaissance squadron, transferred from north China, arrived at Shanghai. The Shigeto Detachment dispersed the enemy on the north side of Kungta airfield, on the outskirts of Shanghai, and from 8 September the squadron used this field jointly with the Navy. It was estimated that the enemy air strength in this area at this time was between 70 and 80 planes. The Japanese Navy had 72 planes in the area, including both land and carrier-based planes. (See Chart No. 2.) The Chinese planes took advantage of moonlight nights and frequently carried out air raids on Shanghai from air bases at Nanching, Chujung, Kuangte and Nanhsiangchen.

In mid-September, the Shanghai Expeditionary Army was reinforced by the 3d Air Brigade headquarters (Maj Gen Tadatsugu Chiga, commander) and two air squadrons and, in mid-October, by two more air squadrons.

When Wangpin airfield (on the outskirts of Shanghai) was almost completed at the end of September, the Army air unit moved there from Kungta. In the final battle for Tachangchen in early October, the 3d Air Brigade cooperated with the Navy air force. The Brigade was charged with the responsibility of conducting reconnaissance, bombing enemy front line positions as well as rear positions and lines

Chart No. 2

The Navy Airplanes Used During China Incident — 1937

Type	Model	Max Speed (kph)	Ceiling (m)	Range (km)	Guns (No x mm)	Bombs (No x kg)	Model Year
Fighter	95	345	10,000	540	2 x 7.7	2 x 30	1930
Fighter	96	426	10,000	850	2 x 7.7	2 x 30	1931
Two Engine Land Based Bomber	96	370	9,110	4,500	2 x 7.7 1 x 20	1 x 800 or 1 x Torpedo	1931
Carrier Dive Bomber	96	300	8,000	1,300	2 x 7.7	1 x 250	1931
Carrier Attack Plane	97	340	6,520	1,700	1 x 7.7	1 x 800 or 1 x Torpedo	1932

Shanghai Base Fighters Type 95 18
               Fighters Type 96 18

               Dive Bombers Type 96 36

                                    72

Taipeh Base Land Based Bombers (M) Type 96 36

of communication. The Brigade's support of the Japanese front line troops contributed greatly to the success of this operation.

During the battle in the vicinity of the Suchou Ho, the 3d Air Brigade reconnoitered enemy positions and assisted the Army in crossing the river. As soon as the Japanese front line troops crossed the Suchou Ho, the Brigade bombed the enemy resisting from prepared positions, greatly assisting in the success of the ground attack.

Immediately after the Tenth Army landed at Hangchou Bay on 5 November, in accordance with an order from the Shanghai Expeditionary Army, the commander of the 3d Air Brigade ordered one air squadron to cooperate with the Tenth Army. Later, by order of the Central China Area Army, this squadron was attached to the Tenth Army. The squadron cooperated with the Tenth Army front line troops in their pursuit action using Wangpin as its base and later, from 1 December, using Changhsing airfield as an advance airfield.

On 7 December, Imperial General Headquarters removed the 3d Air Brigade from the command of the Shanghai Expeditionary Army and placed it under the direct command of the Central China Area Army. It also removed the 3d Air Battalion, the 8th Air Battalion and the 2d Air Company of the 5th Air Battalion from the command of the Provisional Air Group of the North China Area Army and assigned them to the 3d Air Brigade of the Central China Area Army.

During the Nanching Operation in early December, the Central

China Area Army ordered one squadron attached to the Shanghai Expeditionary Army and the main body of the Air Brigade to cooperate with the Tenth Army. The Air Brigade used Wangpin and Lunghuachen airfields as its main bases and Wuchin, Kuangte and Changhsing airfields as its advance bases. It carried out reconnaissance of enemy positions, transported ammunition and provisions by air and made bombing attacks on the Nanching airfield as well as on the castle walls at Nanching. It was particularly successful in attacking troops withdrawing toward the south from the Yangtze River and Wuhu areas.

At the beginning of the Shanghai Operation, the Navy Air Force destroyed the Chinese front line planes but later the enemy reinforced its air strength in this area and frequently carried out counterattacks. From about mid-September the Navy repeatedly attacked enemy air bases near Nanching and again secured air supremacy over the east area of central China. From mid-October the air force bombed Hankou and struck heavy blows against the enemy air force.

During September, the Navy Air Force shot down 32 planes in the vicinity of Nanching. On 2 October, it engaged 36 enemy planes and shot down 13. On 8 October, 9 enemy planes were destroyed on the ground at Hankou and, on the same day, 20 enemy planes were shot down in air combat. On 24 October, three planes were shot down. Later, most of the Chinese planes withdrew from the area.

From the beginning of September, part of the Navy Air Force bombed strategic points at Swatow, Chaoan, the Canton-Kowloon railway and along the Canton-Hankou railway in south China, striking heavy blows at the enemy.

In early October, the Japanese Air Force had secured air supremacy in south China, making it difficult for the Chinese to transport munitions from south China by railway.

GENERAL REFERENCE MAP – CHAPTER 2
MAP NO. 2

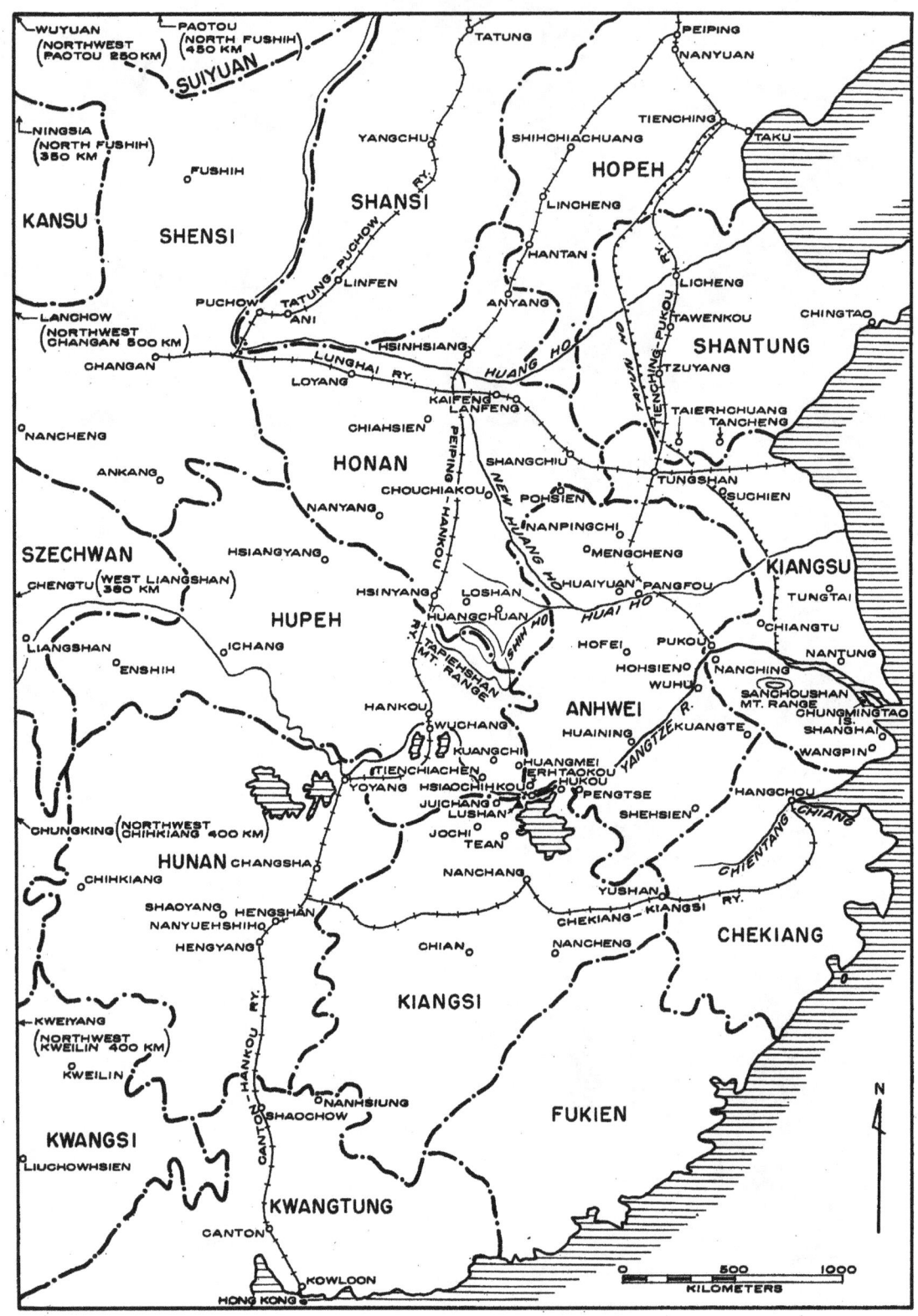

CHAPTER 2

Air Operations in China

1938

Air Operations Prior to the Tungshan Operation

It was estimated that enemy planes in the early part of 1938 numbered between 350 and 450. Half these planes were of Soviet manufacture and, in addition, between 70 and 80 new planes were being imported from Russia each month. Although the Chinese temporarily suspended air operations after the Nanching Operation, in the early part of 1938 they attempted raids against Japanese occupied areas using Lanchow, Changan, Hsiangyang, Hankou, Nanchang and Nancheng as third-line airfields (base airfields); Chiahsien, Hsinyang and Yushan as second-line airfields (used as departure points by bomber units and as standby fields by fighter units) and Loyang, Chouchiakou, Hofei and Shehsien as first-line fields. In addition, they used many advance fields in front of the first-line airfields.

Instructions in regard to the destruction of the enemy air force were the same as the preceding year: the Army was responsible for operations in north China and the Navy for operations in central and south China.

The strength of the Japanese Army Air Force in China from January to April 1938 was 24 squadrons. Fourteen squadrons (four reconnaissance, three fighter, three light bomber and three heavy bomber squadrons - a provisional long-range reconnaissance squadron organized in China was added later) were stationed in north China while ten squadrons (five reconnaissance, three fighter, one light bomber and one heavy bomber squadron) were placed in central China.

The strength and disposition of air units in China (ground service units omitted) from January to April 1938 is given below:

North China   The Provisional Air Group

        Commander: Lt Gen Baron Yoshitoshi Tokugawa

        Provisional Air Group Headquarters

        1st Battalion (Two reconnaissance squadrons)

        3d Battalion (Two fighter squadrons)

        5th Battalion (light bombers, 1 squadron omitted)

        6th Battalion (Two heavy bomber squadrons)

        7th Battalion (Two reconnaissance squadrons)

        9th Battalion (Two light bomber squadrons)

        3d Independent Air Squadron (heavy bombers)

        9th Independent Air Squadron (fighter)

        Aoki Unit (Previously employed as a long range reconnaissance squadron but officially named the 1st Provisional Independent Air Squadron on 12 March).[1]

---

1. The Aoki Unit (commander, Capt Takeo Aoki) was equipped with new Headquarters reconnaissance planes Type "97". One of the prototype planes (Kamikaze) of the "Type 97" accomplished the first Tokyo-London flight on April 1937, and established a world record by flying 15,357 km in 94 hours 17 minutes and 56 seconds.

Central China   The 3d Air Brigade

         Commander: Maj Gen Tadatsugu Chiga

            3d Air Brigade Headquarters

            2d Battalion (Two reconnaissance squadrons)

            One Squadron of the 5th Battalion (light bomber)

            8th Battalion (Two fighter squadrons)

            4th Independent Air Squadron (reconnaissance)

            6th Independent Air Squadron (reconnaissance)

            10th Independent Air Squadron (fighter)

            11th Independent Air Squadron (reconnaissance)

            15th Independent Air Squadron (heavy bomber)

South China (Including Formosa)   As the 4th Air Brigade Headquarters was included in the order of battle of the Fifth Army,[2] it was transferred to Formosa in December 1937. However, with the suspension of the Canton Operation and deactivation of the Fifth Army, on 18 February, by order of Imperial General Headquarters, the Brigade was placed under the command of the Provisional Air Group.

Initially, the Japanese Air Force used Yangchu, Shihchiachuang and Licheng as air bases in north China and later established a base at Anyang. With the progress of operations front line bases were established at Linfen, Ani, Hsinhsiang and Lincheng. Meanwhile, base airfields were established in central China near Nanching and in

---

    2. Monograph No. 180, <u>South China Area Operations Record, 1937 - 1941</u>, Chapter 1.

Hangchou and, as operations progressed, front line bases were established at Chiangtu, Wuhu, Pangfou and Tungtai.

Air Operations in North China

In compliance with an order received from the North China Area Army commander on 10 January to support the Second Army with an element while its main force cooperated with the First Army and destroyed enemy air forces disposed along the Lunghai railway, the Provisional Air Group commander ordered the Nakahira Unit (composed of two reconnaissance squadrons) to continue to render support to the Second Army; the Yamase Unit (commanded by Col Masao Yamase and composed of three and a half squadrons including half a reconnaissance squadron, one fighter squadron and two light bomber squadrons) to support the divisions of the First Army in Shansi Province from the Yangchu airfield; and the Giga Air Brigade (commanded by Maj Gen Tetsuji Giga and composed of seven and a half squadrons including one and a half reconnaissance, two fighter, one light bomber and three heavy bomber squadrons) to support, from Anyang and Hantan airfields, the First Army forces in the Peiping-Hankou railway area as well as to destroy enemy air strength along the Lunghai railway.

Prior to the Hopeh Operation[3] the Provisional Air Group had been engaged chiefly in terrain reconnaissance and in reconnoitering

---

3. Monograph No. 178, North China Area Operations Record, July 1937 - May 1941, Chapter 2.

the enemy situation for the First Army but, with the opening of this operation the Giga Air Brigade bombed enemy strategic positions in the rear, especially railway bridges across the Huang Ho, trains and convoys, and disrupted the enemy's lines of communication. The Brigade also supported the 14th Division and later the 108th Division. Subsequently, when the enemy was put to route, the Brigade bombed enemy troops retreating across the Huang Ho and from the Linfen sector. Following this action, it attacked and bombed enemy forces stationed along the Tatung-Puchow railway. The Yamase Unit supported the actions of the 20th and 109th Divisions.

Prior to the commencement of operations against the Great Canal line[4] by the Second Army in mid-March, the Commander in Chief of the North China Area Army ordered the Group commander to reinforce the air strength in the Second Army sector. Accordingly, the Tawenkou airfield (approximately 80 kilometers south of Licheng) was established and four heavy bombers were stationed there and attached to the Nakahira Unit. As the enemy continued to reinforce its ground force in this sector, during the latter part of March the Group commander added one light bomber squadron and a section of a fighter unit to the air strength already supporting the Second Army's operation.

Although the Chinese Air Force had not been active prior to mid-

---

4. The Tayun Ho was sometimes referred to as the "Great Canal": "Ta" means great and "yun" means canal.

January 1938, toward the end of that month it became quite aggressive. Further, a report was received that it planned to attack Peiping on New Year's Day (lunar calendar). Therefore, late in January, the Provisional Air Group seized the initiative and attacked Loyang, Linfen, Tungshan and Shangchiu airfields. On 30 January the Giga Air Brigade shot down 12 enemy planes over Loyang airfield, causing the enemy to abandon its plan to attack Peiping. Although enemy planes again became active from mid-February, the Provisional Air Group did not attempt any positive counterattack as it was then busily engaged in supporting the Hopeh Operation, but, by early March, when this operation began to draw to a close, the Group was able to concentrate its forces on destroying enemy air strength. It organized the combined fighter-bomber attack units under its direct command into the 1st Air Unit, commanded by Col Yamase and composed mainly of one fighter and two light bomber squadrons and the 2d Air Unit commanded by Col Ryuichi Torida, composed mainly of two fighter and two heavy bomber squadrons. On 8 March these units attacked and inflicted heavy damage on Hsiangyang and Changan airfields. At this time, the Provisional Air Group received an intelligence report stating that the enemy air unit was planning to abandon Changan airfield. The Group, considering it necessary to destroy this force, attacked the airfield on the 11th and 14th with considerable success (five enemy planes were shot down on the 11th). As soon as the 4th Air Brigade Headquarters (commanded by Maj Gen Tomo Fujita and attached to the Provisional

Air Group on 18 February) arrived at Anyang in mid-March, the Group commander placed the attack units which were under his direct command, under the 4th Air Brigade and ordered the Brigade to operate from airfields in and around Anyang and to destroy enemy air planes whenever they were encountered. At the same time, the Brigade was ordered to cooperate with the Japanese ground forces.

Air Operations in Central China

In accordance with Central China Area Army orders, the 3d Air Brigade was attacking enemy forces along the Chientang Chiang and in the Chekiang-Kiangsi railway sector from airfields around Hangchou when the Area Army commander received information that enemy air units were withdrawing to Hsinyang from the Tienching-Pukou railway sector. He, therefore, ordered the Brigade to suspend attacks in the Chekiang-Kiangsi railway area and to attack enemy forces stationed along the Lunghai and Tienching-Pukou railways. About 3 January, the 3d Air Brigade was ordered to prepare for attacks against enemy forces located in the districts along the Lunghai railway west of Tungshan and along the Tienching-Pukou railway south of this town. It was also to be responsible for air defense in the areas surrounding Nanching as well as to be prepared to attack strategic points in this area.

The commander of the 3d Air Brigade dispatched one reconnaissance squadron to the Shanghai Expeditionary Army and another to the

Tenth Army. He assembled the main force of the Brigade, consisting of seven squadrons, at airfields near Nanching and charged a fighter squadron with the responsibility for the air defense of Hangchou. On 4 January, attacks were made on enemy airfields along the Tienching-Pukou railway, on enemy troop movements in the area and on enemy rafts - all with favorable results.

From 1 February, the 3d Air Brigade supported the advance of the 13th Division (Shanghai Expeditionary Army) toward the banks of the Huai Ho and attacked the enemy retreating by land and sea.

About the end of January, the enemy confronting the Tenth Army gradually became more active and it was learned that they were preparing airfields in south Chekiang and Anhwei Provinces. After 10 February, therefore, the commander of the 3d Air Brigade, in accordance with an Area Army order, suspended operations along the Tienching-Pukou railway and transferred the main force of the reconnaissance and bomber units to the Hangchou airfield. From mid-February, the chief mission of this force was to cooperate in the mopping-up operation of the 18th Division and to attack enemy airfields and strategic positions along the Chekiang-Kiangsi railway.

In order to assist in the mopping-up operations in Kuangte and the surrounding area, from mid-March the 3d Air Brigade was ordered to cooperate with the ground operations of the 3d, 6th and 18th Divisions as well as the Hata Detachment, with its reconnaissance unit (two squadrons) an element of its bomber unit (one light and one heavy bomber squadron) and one fighter squadron. It was also made responsible for guarding the lines of communication between the Army headquarters and the various groups. In addition, it was ordered to use part of its reconnaissance unit to cooperate with the 101st Division's operation to capture Nantung and Chungmingtao Island. The remaining units of the Air Brigade were to assume responsibility for the defense of Nanching.

Although its cooperation with other ground units was suspended on 1 April, the Air Brigade, on 7 April, sent part of its force to assist the 3d Division to the north of Sanchoushan Mountain Range and the Sato Detachment of the 101st Division along the left bank of the Yangtze River. The Brigade also was charged with the responsibility of gathering intelligence to aid the Army's operational plans for an attack against Tungshan and preparations for participation in the operation.

From the beginning of the year the Brigade had been unsuccessful in repulsing enemy air attacks on the airfields at Nanching, Wuhu and Hangchou due to the fact that the Russian-made planes used by the Chinese were superior to the Type 95 then being used by the Brigade. In mid-March, however, the Brigade was reinforced by a few Type 97 fighters. These proved helpful in shooting down enemy planes. Between January and April the Brigade made approximately twelve raids.

In January two enemy planes were shot down, in March three and April six.

Air Operations During the Battle of Tungshan

Although no operational boundary between the Provisional Air Group of the North China Area Army and the 3d Air Brigade of the Central China Expeditionary Army was defined for the general attack on Tungshan, boundaries for patrols were established along the line connecting Tungshan, Shangchiu, Chouchiakou and Hsinyang.

As a result of negotiations between the Army and Navy, the Navy Air Force assumed responsibility for the region extending from the area along the Lunghai railway, east of the line connecting Tancheng (110 km east-northeast of Tungshan) and Suchien (70 km south of Tancheng) to the area south of the line connecting Hohsien (50 km southwest of Nanching) and Chouchiakou. They were to attack enemy airfields in this sector and also to destroy enemy reinforcements being transported along the Tienching-Pukou railway.

At the beginning of April, when the battle near Taierhchuang was at its height, the commander of the North China Area Army ordered the Provisional Air Group commander to reduce the force cooperating with the ground operations in the area west of the Peiping-Hankou railway and replenish the strength supporting the Second Army.

The Group commander, therefore, ordered the Terakura Air Brigade (three reconnaissance, one fighter and one light bomber squadron, commanded by Maj Gen Shozo Terakura, who succeeded Maj Gen Giga on 9 March) to be deployed in the area along the Tienching-Pukou railway to support the Second Army and also to cooperate with the Fujita Air Brigade (4th Air Brigade composed of two reconnaissance, four fighter and two heavy bomber squadrons) in destroying enemy air strength penetrating the area along the Lunghai railway from Lanfeng and the area to the east. At the same time, the Fujita Air Brigade was ordered to destroy enemy air strength located in the vicinity of the Peiping-Hankou railway as well as to support the operations of the First Army and, when necessary, those of the Second Army.

The Terakura Air Brigade in the Tienching-Pukou railway zone concentrated its main strength (10th Air Regiment) at Tzuyang.[5] The Fujita Air Brigade in the Peiping-Hankou railway zone stationed its main strength at Anyang with one fighter squadron in Shansi Province. From here the Brigades supported the Seya and Sakamoto Detachments and later cooperated in reorganizing the battle line. They also supported the Second Army's counteroffensive after 18 April. At the same time, the Fujita Brigade attacked the enemy air force near Changan destroying a number of enemy planes.[6]

---

5. The 10th Air Regiment, dispatched from the Kwantung Army, reached Nanyuan on 15 April when the commander of the Provisional Air Group assigned it to the Terakura Air Brigade. At the end of June, this Regiment was returned to the Kwantung Army.

6. Although the exact number of planes destroyed at Changan is unknown, the total number destroyed from 4 April to 5 July was 34 planes shot down and 4 destroyed on the ground. Planes destroyed at Changan were included in this report.

In late April, the Provisional Air Group received orders from the North China Area Army to use its main strength to support the battle for Tungshan by cooperating with the ground forces' advance toward the Lunghai railway. Emphasis was placed on the importance of supporting the Second Army's operation and of maintaining close contact with the 3d Air Brigade (under the command of the Central China Area Army) and the Navy air units.

The Provisional Air Group cooperated with the operations of the Second Army and the 14th Division (1st Army)[7] without much change in the distribution of its strength.

About mid-May, when the Chinese in the area around Tungshan began to retreat, the Air Group, acting on orders from the North China Area Army, used its main strength to bomb the retreating enemy and also enemy trains running west on the Lunghai railway, inflicting heavy casualties and much damage. In addition, the Group supported the 14th Division in the occupation of Lanfeng. Later, when the Division was surrounded by a superior enemy force, the Group rendered great assistance by transporting provisions by air and bombing the enemy. In mid-June, when the 14th and 16th Divisions were isolated on the edge of areas which had been flooded when the enemy destroyed the banks of the Huang Ho, the Group carried out reconnaissance of

---

7. The 14th Division was attached to the Second Army during the Tungshan Operation from 2 June to 13 June.

the flooded areas, transported provisions by air and bombed the enemy, thus facilitating the withdrawal of the divisions.

In the middle of April, the Central China Expeditionary Army made the following agreement with the Navy Air Force in regard to the Tungshan Operation:

> Bombing and reconnoitering in cooperation with the Army advancing to the east of the 13th Division's line of advance will be chiefly the responsibility of the Army air units.
>
> The air base of the Navy Air Unit will be Nanching, but, when necessary, naval aircraft may land at Pangfou.
>
> Air to air battles will be fought chiefly by the Navy Air Unit.
>
> In order to cooperate with ground operations, preparations will be made by the Navy Air Unit to attack the enemy on the left flank of the 3d, 6th and 13th Divisions, to bomb important enemy rear points, troops and positions, and also to cooperate with the forces east of the Tienching-Pukou railway by carrying out bombing operations, when necessary.

On 17 April, the 3d Air Brigade commander concentrated his main strength in the Pangfou-Nanching sector and used this force to support the divisions fighting along the Tienching-Pukou railway. Elements were stationed at Hangchou and Wuhu to reconnoiter the enemy situation on the southern front and to cooperate with the ground forces in the area. At the same time, preparations were made to destroy enemy air strength.

While these preparations were being completed, the Air Brigade did not carry out any bombing raids but reconnoitered the enemy situation and terrain continuously. On 5 May, when the ground forces began advancing from the banks of the Huai Ho, the Air Brigade cooperated with the 9th and 13th Divisions in capturing Mengcheng and multiple enemy positions northwest of Huaiyuan. After the 12th, the Air Brigade supported the 3d Division's attack against strong enemy positions near Nanpingchi and also supported the attack of the main body of the Army against enemy positions west of Tungshan. From the middle of May, when the enemy began to retreat, the Brigade bombed the enemy in flight, inflicting many casualties.

During this operation the Brigade reported shooting down five enemy planes over Pangfou and Wuhu on 30 April, destroying five more on the Pohsien airfield on 11 May and shooting down one enemy plane which came to raid Mengcheng on 20 May.

Operations to annihilate enemy strength before, during and after the Tungshan Operation were carried out on 4 April, 10 April, 20 May and 5 July against the Changan and Hsinyang airfields and in the areas around Shangchiu and east of Lanfeng. During these engagements a total of 34 enemy planes were destroyed (four planes on the ground) and several hangars were bombed and destroyed.

Air Operations During the Wu-Han Operation
Reorganization and Order of Battle of Air Group

During the latter part of July 1938 the formation of air units was revised. The main points of this revision were:

    a. In the past an air battalion had been composed of fighting and maintenance divisions. In order to concentrate fighting divisions primarily for battle, fighting and maintenance were to be separated. Fighting divisions were organized into air regiments while airfield battalions were charged with the responsibility of maintenance, guard, supply of ammunition, provisions etc. This was known as the "Air and Ground Separation Plan."

    In addition, a headquarters was established to control the airfield battalions and other ground units.

    b. The name "Air Battalion" was changed to "Air Regiment."

    c. The name "Provisional Air Group" was changed to "Air Group."

    d. In the past, the Air Brigade had functioned only as an administrative headquarters. Now, its order of battle was issued by Imperial General Headquarters and a regiment (three squadrons) was placed under the direct command of the Brigade.

    On 2 August, the order of battle of the Air Group in China was published to become effective on 6 August. (Chart No. 3)

Preparations for Wu-Han Operation

    Immediately after the Tungshan Operation, the Central China Expeditionary Army began to prepare for the invasion of Hankou by advancing the 6th Division and the Hata Detachment along the left bank and on the waters of the Yangtze River. During this advance the 3d

Chart No. 3

Outline of Order of Battle of the Air Group in China   6 August 1938

Army	Group	Air Brigade	Air Forces — Air Regiment (squadrons)					Ground Units (Number of units)
			Reconnaissance	Fighter	Light bomber	Heavy bomber	Total number of squadrons	
Central China Expeditionary Army	Air Group (Commander: Lt Gen Baron Yoshitoshi Tokugawa)	1st Air Bgd; (Commander Maj Gen Shozo, Terakura)	16th Independent Air Squadron	77th Air Regt	31st Air Regt		5	Air sector headquarters (2)
		3d Air Bgd; (Commander Maj Gen Chuji, Chiga)	17th Independent Air Squadron	10th Independent Air Squadron	45th and 75th Air Regts		6	Airfield battalion (7)
								Airfield company (2)
		4th Air Bgd; (Commander Maj Gen Tomo, Fujita)		64th Air Regt (-3d Squadron)		60th and 98th Air Regts	6	Air signal unit (1)
								Field antiaircraft artillery unit (4)
								Field searchlight unit (1)
		Directly assigned to the Air Group	18th Independent Air Squadron				1	Motor transport company (7)
								Land duty unit (6)
		Total number of squadrons	3	5	6	4	18	Field air depot (2)

50

Chart No. 3

Outline of Order of Battle of the Air Group in China (cont'd)

Army Group	Air Brigade	Air Forces					Ground Units (Number of units)
		Air Regiment (squadrons)				Total number of squadrons	
		Reconnaissance	Fighter	Light bomber	Heavy bomber		
North China Area Army	North China Area Army Air Unit (Commander: Col Einosuke, Sudo Later Maj Gen Hisao, Hozoji)		3d Squadron (64th Air Regt)	27th and 30th Air Regts		5	Air sector headquarters (2) Airfield battalion (2) Air signal unit (1) Air intelligence unit (1) Field antiaircraft artillery unit (1) Motor transport company (1) Land duty unit (1)

51

Brigade cooperated with both the 6th Division and the Navy Air Group and played a large part in the capture of Huaining, Pengtse, Hukou and Hsiaochihkou.

Although the 3d Air Brigade was attached to the Air Group on 5 August, it continued to carry out its former duties while the Group assembled. Its main strength cooperated with the Eleventh Army and an element supported the Second Army's operation.

Immediately after the commander of the Air Group had received orders from the commander of the North China Area Army on 6 July to prepare for the invasion of Hankou, he had prepared to establish a command post at Nanching on 23 July. As soon as the Air Group was attached to the Central China Expeditionary Army, however, on 6 August the Air Group commander received orders to advance his main strength to central China as early as possible, by plane or by ship. At the same time, the 3d Air Brigade in central China was ordered to continue its duties as in the past.

Accordingly, ground service units first arrived in central China to expedite the preparation of airfields and air units were then disposed to begin their maneuvers. Work to complete the construction of airfields at Wangpin, Hangchou, Nanching, Hofei, Huaining and Pengtse was accelerated.

The commander of the Air Group planned the basic disposition of his forces as follows: Headquarters and 18th Independent Reconnaissance Squadron at Nanching; 1st Air Brigade at Hofei and Huaining or, if necessary, at Pangfou; 3d Air Brigade at Pengtse and Huaining (earlier at Huangmei and Hsiaochihkou), and the 4th Air Brigade at Pengtse, Nanching, Hangchou and Wangpin. At this time the units in north China, which were under the command of the Air Group commander, were at Anyang and Shangchiu with elements at Licheng, Tungshan and Nanyuan. As the Huai Ho railway bridge had been washed away, most of the ground forces from north China were transported by sea from Chingtao or Taku while the air units were transported by air. By the end of August the concentration of the main strength of the Air Group and the planned deployment had been completed.

Summary of Air Operations During the Wu-Han Operation

In order to capture Wuchang and Hankou, on 22 August the commander of the Central China Expeditionary Army ordered the Air Group commander to use his main strength to support the Eleventh Army and an element to support the Second Army. At the same time, the Air Group was ordered to cooperate with the Navy Air Group in destroying the enemy's air power and attacking strategic targets in the areas affected by the projected operation.

In compliance with these orders, on 26 August the Air Group commander ordered the 1st Air Brigade (one reconnaissance squadron, two fighter squadrons and two light bomber squadrons) to support the Second Army's operation; the 3d Air Brigade (one reconnaissance squadron, one fighter squadron and four light bomber squadrons) to support the Eleventh Army's operation and, at the same time, destroy the enemy air force in action against the Eleventh Army. The 3d Air Brigade was then to advance to Erhtaokou to the north of Hsiaochihkou. The 4th Air Brigade (two fighter squadrons and four heavy bomber squadrons) was deployed at strategic points behind both the Second and Eleventh Armies to assist when required.

The Navy Air Group during August had continually attacked enemy airfields at Hankou, Nanchang, Chian, Ichang, Changsha, Hengyang, Shaoyang, Liuchowhsien, Shaochow and Nanhsiung and had succeeded in neutralizing enemy air power in this area.

As the Air Group commander gave first priority to the support of ground operations, aggressive action was not undertaken against enemy air power unless enemy action against the ground forces was anticipated.

The ground crews of the Air Group were divided roughly into the right sector (one air sector headquarters and two airfield battalions) and left sector (one air sector headquarters and five airfield battalions) in the Second and Eleventh Armies theaters of operation respectively.

In order to support the Second Army's operation, the 1st Air Brigade moved to Hofei on 25 August and Huangchuan on 29 September. At first, the main forces of the 3d Air Brigade supported the Eleventh Army's operation with an element supporting the Second Army from airfields at Huaining and Pengtse. After 26 August, however, the Air Brigade moved to the airfield at Erhtaokou and concentrated on supporting the Eleventh Army. On 29 August, the 4th Air Brigade moved to bases at Nanching and Hangchou and from there bombed the enemy facing the Eleventh Army. They bombed enemy entrenched around Kuangchi and Tienchiachen and enemy positions located at the western and southern bases of Mt Lushan. When the Eleventh Army was engaged in battle with the enemy in the vicinity of Juichang and Jochi, the Air Brigade supported it with heavy bombings. When the 106th Division was surrounded by the enemy northwest of Tean, the 4th Air Brigade, in cooperation with the 3d Air Brigade, bombed the encircling enemy and supplied the Division with food from the air. Part of the 4th Air Brigade also cooperated with the 1st Air Brigade in supporting the Second Army's operation along the Shih Ho, the invasion of Huangchuan and the bombing of Loshan and Hsinyang.

At the beginning of October, the 4th Air Brigade (4th Air Brigade headquarters, 64th Air Regiment, less the 3d Squadron, and the 31st Air Regiment)[8] was placed in the order of battle of the Twenty-first Army and, about mid-October, moved to Canton. The Air Group commander then placed the 60th and 98th Air Regiments under the com-

---

8. As the 4th Air Brigade did not possess any light bomber units, the 31st Air Regiment was transferred to the Brigade just prior to its transfer to the Twenty-first Army.

mand of the 3d Air Brigade. As the 4th Air Brigade did not arrive in the area in time to participate in the Canton Operation, the Navy Air Unit supported the Twenty-first Army during this operation.

Not only did the Air Group support the Second Army during the Tapiehshan Mountains Penetration Operation (28 Sep - 29 Oct 1938) and the Eleventh Army's campaign to cut the Canton-Hankou railway (22 - 27 Oct) but it also attacked and inflicted severe casualties on the retreating enemy.

From 9 September, in order to nullify the enemy's air power, the Navy Air Unit bombed the airfields at Nanchang, Chian and Yushan and, in late September, bombed airfields at Hengyang, Kweiyang, Chungking and Liangshan. In spite of this, at the end of September, enemy aircraft appeared over the operational zone of the Second Army and, from early October, repeatedly attacked this area. As a countermeasure, on 4 October, the 4th Air Brigade attacked Hankou but no enemy planes were found. On 18 October, the 1st Air Brigade attacked Nanyang and, on the 19th, the 3d Air Brigade raided Changsha with some success. After moving to the airfield near Hankou in early November, the main force of the Air Group raided Hengyang and destroyed sixteen enemy planes on the ground. It also raided Hengshan and Nanyuehshih, southwest of Hengshan, on 7, 8 and 9 November.

Air Operations Over North China to Support the Wu-Han Operation

After the Tungshan Operation, the North China Area Army was charged primarily with keeping peace and order in the occupied areas.

In early August, when the North China Area Army Air Unit[9] was organized, the Area Army commander ordered the Sudo Unit (one fighter squadron and two light bomber squadrons)[10] to Anyang and Tungshan with the mission of gathering enemy intelligence and supporting the ground operations of the 1st Army garrison groups (the 5th and 114th Divisions and the 5th Independent Mixed Brigade garrisoning Shantung Province and the area around Tungshan, the 110th Division guarding the Peiping-Tienching sector and the Cavalry Group on the east side of the New Huang Ho). The Yamase Unit (two light bomber squadrons)[11] was stationed at Yangchu and Tatung to support the land operations

---

9. The Order of Battle of the North China Area Army Air Unit was published on 2 August 1938. The unit was composed of the 3d squadron of the 64th Air Regiment, 27th Air Regiment, 90th Air Regiment and two airfield battalions.

10. The original Japanese manuscript states that the Sudo Unit was composed of three air reconnaissance squadrons. This is incorrect. The Unit, which was commanded by Col Einosuke Sudo, was composed of the 3d Squadron, 64th Air Regiment (one fighter squadron) and the 27th Air Regiment (two light bomber squadrons).

11. The 90th Air Regiment (two light bomber squadrons) was commanded by Colonel Masao Yamase.

of the First Army and the Mongolia Garrison Army in that area.[12]

In mid-September, one light bomber squadron[13] and part of the airfield battalion of the North China Area Army Air Unit was attached to the Twenty-first Army.[14] On 22 September, the 15th Air Regiment (two reconnaissance squadrons), the 12th Air Regiment (two heavy bomber squadrons) and two airfield battalions from the Kwantung Army were placed under the tactical command of the North China Area Army commander. The Area Army commander ordered the North China Area Army Air Unit to support the operations of the First Army and the Mongolia Garrison Army, and the 15th Air Regiment to support the 114th and 21st Divisions, the Cavalry Group and the 5th Independent Mixed Brigade. The 12th Air Regiment was stationed at Anyang and ordered to attack and disrupt railway communications along the western section of the Lunghai railway and the southern section of the Peiping-Hankou railway.

In the Northern Shansi Province Operation carried out from late September, the main force of the North China Area Army Air Unit sup-

---

12. The North China Area Army commander divided the ground units of the Air Unit into the east and west group. The East Group was charged with maintenance on airfields at Peiping, Tienching, Licheng, Tungshan and Shangchiu and the West Group with maintenance at airfields at Shihchiachuang, Anyang, Hsinhsiang, Yangchu, Linfen and Ani.

13. The basic Japanese manuscript states that one air reconnaissance squadron was transferred. This is an error. It was a light bomber squadron.

14. The Twenty-first Army was organized in mid-September for the Canton Operation. Monograph No. 180, South China Area Operations Record, 1937 - 1941, Chapter 1.

ported the First Army and the Mongolia Garrison Army operations while the 15th Air Regiment, from Nanyuan, supported mainly the 110th Division's operation. The 12th Air Regiment supported the operations in the Wu-Han sector by attacking the area along the Peiping-Hankou railway.

On 6 October, the 7th Air Brigade Headquarters, commanded by Maj Gen Hisao Hozoji, was transferred from the Kwantung Army and placed under the command of the North China Area Army commander. The Area Army commander then placed the air units in north China under the command of the Brigade Headquarters with orders to continue their original missions.

Upon receiving an intelligence report that with the fall of Wuchang and Hankou, the main force of the enemy air force was retreating to the west and concentrating at Lanchow, the Air Brigade commander, in compliance with an Area Army order, prepared to destroy the enemy air power in that area. From the middle to the end of November, the main force of the Air Brigade, using Paotou and Ani as its bases, bombed Lanchow continuously while an element carried out bombing raids against Ningsia, Wuyuan, Changan and Fushih.

Air Operations After the Occupation of Wu-Han

After the fall of Yoyang on 11 November, the Air Group commander ordered part of the 1st Air Brigade to reconnoiter the enemy situation northwest of the Second Army; part of the 3d Air Brigade to reconnoiter southwest of the Eleventh Army and part of the 18th Independent Air Squadron to reconnoiter the area to the rear of the enemy forces. At this time, the Air Group commander concentrated the fighters and heavy bombers of the 3d Air Brigade at Hankou under the tactical command of the commander of the 1st Air Brigade.

On 17 November, the 12th Air Regiment and one airfield battalion were transferred from the North China Area Army to the Central China Expeditionary Army. At the same time, Imperial General Headquarters ordered the 1st Air Brigade (Brigade Headquarters, 10th, 16th and 18th Independent Squadrons, and the 60th and 98th Air Regiments), the 3d Air Brigade (Brigade Headquarters, 17th Independent Squadron and the 77th, 45th and 75th Air Regiments) and other units from the Air Group to be placed under the command of the Central China Expeditionary Army. The remaining air units of the North China Area Army Air Unit (7th Air Brigade Headquarters, 3/64th Air Regiment, 27th Air Regiment (minus one squadron), 90th Air Regiment, 15th Air Regiment and other small units were organized into the new North China Area Army Air Unit and placed in the order of battle of the North China Area Army. This unit continued to support the operations of the various units in north China.

On 2 December, in an attempt to suppress and crush the remaining anti-Japanese faction and secure the occupied areas, Imperial General Headquarters ordered offensive air operations to be undertaken in north and central China, the objectives being the destruction of Chinese air power as well as political and strategical centers. All Army air units were instructed to cooperate closely with the Navy Air Force.

At this time, Imperial General Headquarters issued an Army-Navy Agreement in regard to air operations over China, the main essentials of which were:

>Operational Policy:
>
>>Throughout important areas in China the Army and Navy air groups will combine to carry out strategic air operations aimed at breaking the enemy's will to resist.
>>
>>The Army air units will directly support land operations and the Navy will support operations at sea.
>
>Strategically and Politically Effective Air Operations:
>
>>The Army Air Group will be charged with the responsibility of strategic and political air operations chiefly in the strategic areas of central and north China. The Navy Air Group will be responsible chiefly for strategic and political areas in central and south China.
>>
>>Army and Navy air strengths may be distributed according to the exigencies of the circumstances.
>>
>>In order to carry out strategic and political air operations China will be divided as follows:
>>
>>>North China: Shantung, Honan, Shensi and Kansu Provinces.

South China: Fukien, Kwangtung, Kwangsi and Yunnan Provinces.

Central China: The area between north and south China.

Direct Cooperation with Ground or Sea Operations:

The Army will cooperate directly with ground operations and the Navy with sea operations. However, they may be reinforced, depending upon the situation.

Strength:

Distribution of strength is shown on Chart No. 4.

In accordance with an agreement between the Central China Expeditionary Army and the North China Area Army, the latter was to supply the necessary assistance when the Air Group used airfields at Paotou, Ani and Anyang for operations against north China (Suiyuan, Ningsia, Kansu, Shensi and Honan Provinces). On 9 December, the commander of the Central China Expeditionary Army ordered the Air Group, in cooperation with the Navy, to conduct aggressive air operations over north and central China to neutralize military and political strategic centers and destroy the enemy's air strength.

About the beginning of November, enemy air strength was estimated to be about 40 squadrons with 340 planes, half of which were fighter planes. Their bases were at Lanchow, Nancheng, Chungking, Chihkiang and Liuchowhsien with Changan, Ankang, Liangshan, Enshih, Hengyang and Chian as front line bases. Toward the middle of the month, the enemy air force began a general withdrawal to the west.

On 20 December, Lt Gen Eijiro Ebashi, commander of the Air Group, planned to attack the enemy air forces in central China from Hankou and those in north China from Paotou and Ani. He, therefore, ordered the 1st Air Brigade, with the 12th and 59th Air Regiments attached, to attack enemy air strength in central China as well as the important enemy strategic and political centers from 24 December until mid-January. At the same time he ordered the 3d Air Brigade to continue to support the Eleventh Army's operations but, when required, to cooperate with the 1st Air Brigade in attacking enemy airfields and important positions in central China. Although the 1st Air Brigade raided Chungking on 26 December and Chihkiang on the 29th, the results were unsatisfactory due to bad weather conditions.

Meanwhile, the 7th Air Brigade cooperated with the North China Area Army's operations and, at the same time, maintained airfields at Paotou and Ani in preparation for the planned air offensive in north China by the Air Group. The 4th Air Brigade (1st Direct Cooperation Air Unit, 1st Air Squadron of the 27th Air Regiment, 31st Air Regiment and 64th Air Regiment, less 3d squadron) commanded by Maj Gen Tomo Fujita, which was attached to the Twenty-first Army, completed its concentration near Canton on 20 November. It then cooperated with the punitive operations of the 18th and 104th Divisions.

Chart No. 4

Distribution of Army and Navy Air Strength
2 December 1938

Area		Group or Unit	Reconnaissance plane	Fighter	Light bomber	Heavy bomber	Total	Total (Navy and Army)
Central China	Army	Air Group — 1st Air Brigade	18	12		30	60	
		3d Air Brigade	9	24	45		78	
		59th Air Regiment		20			20	
		12th Air Regiment				15	15 / 173	337
	Navy	2d Combined Air Gp		54 (Carrier borne planes)	12 (Carrier borne planes) / 24 (Carrier attack planes)	26 (Medium attack planes)	116	
		1st Combined Air Gp				24 (Medium attack planes)	24	
		3d Air Group	24 (Reconnaissance seaplanes)				24 / 164	
South China	Army	4th Air Brigade	13	24	18		55 / 55	141
	Navy	1st Carrier Division		9	6 (Carrier borne planes) / 18 (Carrier attack planes)		33	
		14th Carrier Division		12	6 (Carrier borne planes) / 18 (Carrier borne planes)		36	
		Takao Air Unit				9 (Medium attack planes)	9	
		Seaplane tender	3 (Reconnaissance seaplanes)				8 / 86	

Chart No. 4

Distribution of Army and Navy Air Strength (cont'd)

Area		Group or Unit	Type and number of airplanes				Total (Navy and Army)
			Reconnaissance plane	Fighter	Light bomber	Heavy bomber	Total
North China	Army	Headquarters of 7th Air Brigade						
		3d Squadron of 64th Air Regiment		12			12	44
		27th Air Regiment (1st squadron omitted)			9		9	
		90th Air Flotilla			18		18/39	
	Navy	Chingtao air unit			5 (Carrier attack planes)		5/5	
Total		Army planes	40	92	90	45	267	522
		Naval planes	32	75	89	59	255	
		Total	72	167	179	104	522	522

In November, the Navy Air Force raided Liangshan, Chihkiang, Kweilin, Chungking and Chengtu and in December, Liuchowhsien. It shot down or destroyed on the ground 70 planes as well as causing considerable damage to important enemy positions.

GENERAL REFERENCE MAP — CHAPTERS 3, 4, 5.
MAP NO. 3

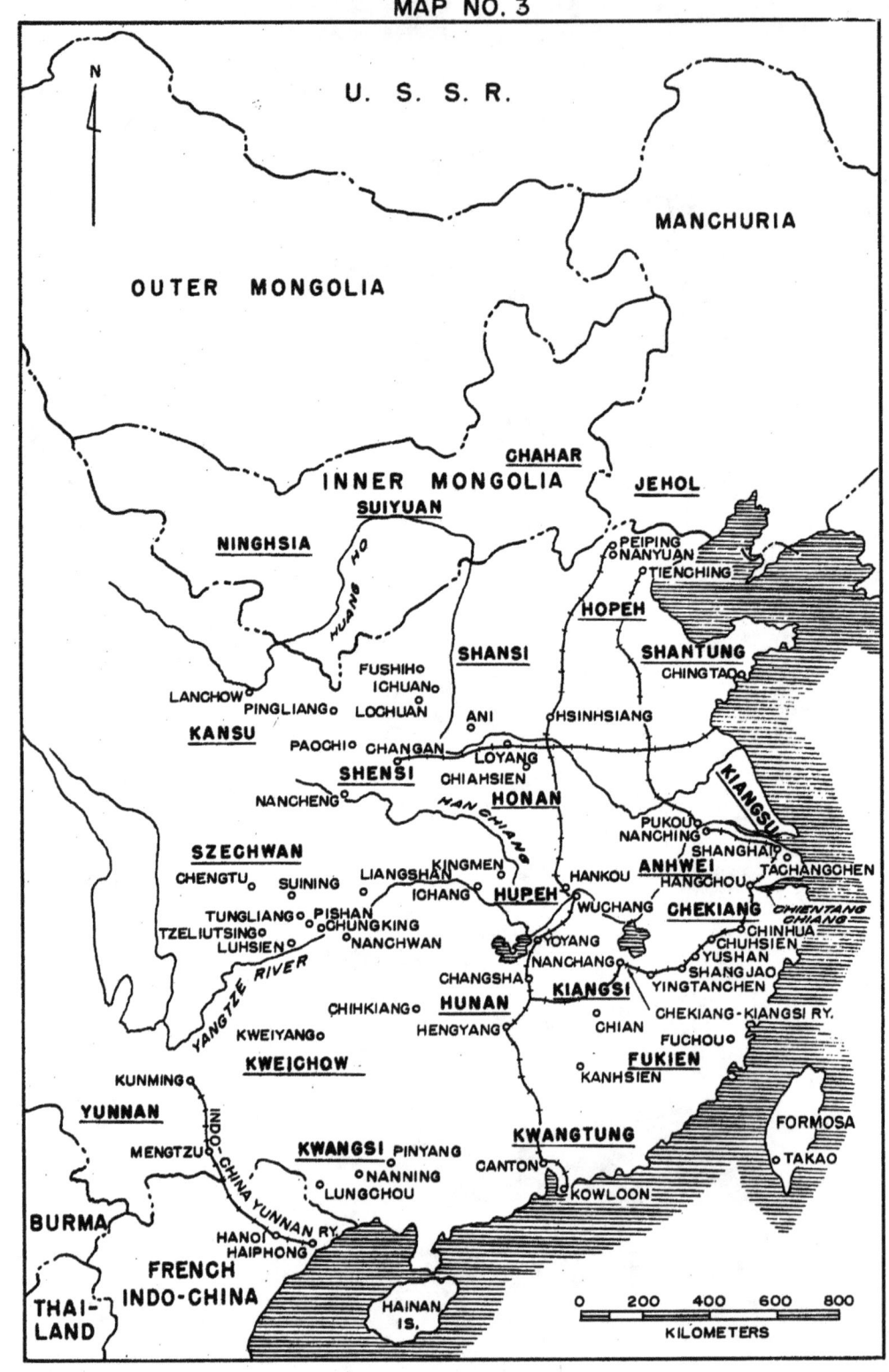

CHAPTER 3

Operations in China

1939

Outline of First Air Operation (24 Dec 38 - 28 Feb 39)

By the end of October 1938, Japanese forces had occupied Canton and the Wuchang-Hankou-Hanyang area. The Army Air Force then cooperated with the ground force in carrying out mopping-up operations from Yoyang to the Han Chiang west of Wuchang. At that time it was considered vitally important to destroy the enemy air strength and neutralize enemy military and political strategic centers. An offensive operation against the interior, therefore, was planned to be undertaken immediately after the occupation of Wu-Han sector. The Army Air Force, however, did not have the planes or the trained personnel to carry out long-distance attacks and the opportunity to enlarge on the success of the Wu-Han Operation was lost.

Although approximately 70 per cent of the regular strength of each air unit was on air service duty, very few of the pilots had been trained to fly at night. The majority of the pilots in the 60th Air Regiment, in which the planes had been changed to Type 97 heavy bombers, were inexperienced in flying this type of plane. Very few of the pilots of the 98th and 12th Air Regiments, which were equipped with Type "I" heavy bombers,[1] were trained to fly at night and the airfields in central China were not suitable for use by heavy bombers for night operations. The 18th Independent Air Squadron, which was the Headquarters reconnaissance squadron, had only two or three pilots able to fly at night, and the Headquarters reconnaissance units and the heavy bomber unit had not been trained to cooperate with one another in attacks.

After the Wu-Han Operation, owing to lack of replacement equipment, the efficiency of the planes (particularly long-distance bombers) decreased considerably. Communications equipment for night flying and navigation methods were faulty and new planes from Japan did not arrive as scheduled.

The striking range of planes used in the operation against the interior of China was:

Type 97 heavy bomber (Model 1):	approx. 800 km (bomb load - 500 kilograms)
Type "I" heavy bomber:	approx. 700 km (bomb load - 500 kilograms)
Type 97 (Headquarters reconnaissance planes):	approx. 900 km
Type 97 fighter:	approx. 400 km

---

1. The Type "I" was an Italian plane, a FIAT BR-20. As the production program of Type 97's was behind schedule, in 1937 the Japanese Army purchased 77 BR-20's from Italy to equip two air regiments. The capacity of these planes was:

Max Sp	Ceiling	Range	Guns	Bombs
392/6560	9,000	3,000	13mm x 1 7.7mm x 1	500kg x 1

Air Bases, Weather Services and Navigation Aids:

In order to successfully carry out operations against the interior, it was necessary to use airfields as near the front lines as possible which were capable of accommodating heavy planes. However, the only fields from which these planes could be launched were at Hankou and Ani and, because of poor navigation aids, communication equipment and billeting facilities, concentration of units on these fields was difficult.

Efforts were made to improve this situation during the last two months of 1938[2] as it was planned to launch an attack in January 1939. The Headquarters of the Air Group assumed responsibility for directing the operation and ordered the 1st Air Brigade (commanded by Maj Gen Shozo Terakura and composed of one reconnaissance squadron, two fighter squadrons and eight heavy bomber squadrons) to carry out the operation.

Outline of Air Operation in Szechwan Province

Preparations for the operation were generally completed by the end of December 1938 when the first attack was launched. Attacks were carried out from the base at Hankou on 26 December 1938 and 7, 10 and 25 January 1939, against the strategically and politically important areas around Chungking. It was difficult, however, to

---

2. This included the training of bomber units.

confirm targets as the skies were so heavily overcast.[3] The only attack carried out under favorable weather conditions was on 10 January when the results were reported as "satisfactory."

During these attacks headquarters reconnaissance planes were used to confirm weather conditions, report on enemy positions and the results of the attacks. Heavy bomber units, protected by a fighter unit on setting out and returning, were used for the attacks. As the enemy air force appeared to lack both fighting spirit and operational skill, later attacks were carried out without fighter protection.

Outline of Air Operation in Lanchow Area

Lanchow was an important point in communications between China and Russia. It was estimated that close to 100 planes (the majority of them made in Russia) were regularly stationed at airfields in the vicinity of this town. The main types of planes were the E-15 and E-16 and many Russians on air duty participated in combat. It was thought that the cutting or threatening of the so-called "Red Route" was of great importance not only in the destruction of the enemy air force in the area but also it would deal a telling blow strategically and politically to Chiang Kai-shek's regime in Chungking.

---

3. The Chinese have a saying that "the dogs bark at the sight of the sun" as it is so rarely seen in this area during the winter.

At the beginning of February, Japanese air attack units were moved to Ani airfield in Shansi Province and prepared to attack Lanchow and Chengtu. On 12, 20 and 22 February the 12th, 60th and 98th Air Regiments (approximately 30 planes) cooperated in attacks against Lanchow. One hundred enemy planes, both in the air and on the ground, were reported damaged during these attacks. At this time it appeared as though the morale of the enemy air force was high and air battles were often carried on for a long period of time. As both the 12th and 98th Air Regiments suffered heavy casualties the attacks were suspended and the air units ordered to assemble in central China to prepare for future operations.

Outline of Second Air Operation (1 Oct 1939 - 31 Oct 1939)

A great many lessons were learnt during the first operation in regard to employment of air units, organization, equipment and training. It was found that if only a few planes from heavy bomber regiments were used in an attack that this was apt to give the enemy a chance to attack them as, in the air, communication and cooperation were very often lost. Further, it was pointed out that while Type "I" heavy bombers were highly inflammable and quickly ignited from a shot from the enemy, their firing equipment was superior to the Type 97 heavy bombers, which were otherwise regarded as better planes.

It was decided, therefore, to reorganize the heavy bomber units into one powerful combined regiment composed of 36 Type 97 heavy bombers and to select, transfer and train the best air crewmen from other air regiments into this unit before opening the next attack.

On 28 April 1939, Imperial General Headquarters reorganized the air force in China and issued directives concerning the preparation and execution of air attack operations and cooperation between the Army and Navy air forces.

Important transfers in this reorganization plan were:

> The Air Group will be removed from the command of the Central China Expeditionary Army commander and returned to the command of the North China Area Army. The 27th Air Regiment in north China will be placed under the direct command of the Air Group commander and the 90th Air Regiment will be placed under the command of the 1st Air Brigade commander. The 3d Air Brigade will be removed from the command of the Air Group and placed under the command of the commander of the Central China Expeditionary Army.
>
> The 7th Air Brigade (Headquarters 7th Air Brigade, 12th and 15th Air Regiments) will be transferred from north China to south China.

Important points in orders in regard to air attack operations were:

> In attacking enemy strategic and political centers, it is necessary to concentrate fighting strength at opportune times and to make special efforts to search out and destroy the supreme command and highest political organs of the enemy.
>
> Attack operations under the command of the commander of the North China Area Army will be carried out after autumn of this year. The unit responsible for these operations will complete its training by this time.

Should it be considered expedient, the commander of the North China Area Army and the commander of the Central China Expeditionary Army may station all or part of their air forces within the zone of operations of other Area Armies.

If necessary, part of the ground service units presently under the command of the Central China Expeditionary Army commander with the concurrence of the commander of the Central China Expeditionary Army, may be placed temporarily under the command of the commander of the North China Area Army.

The commander of the North China Area Army will order the commander of the Air Group to assume responsibility for the organization and supply of air units under the command of the Central China Expeditionary Army. Should it be considered necessary, the commander of the North China Area Army may order the commander of the Air Group to command these units.

If necessary, the commander of the Central China Expeditionary Army may assign to the commander of the Air Group the responsibility for supply, equipment and organization of supply facilities for the air force in its area of operation and also the responsibility for guard duty and logistics of the air force under the command of the North China Area Army commander.

Furthermore, this agreement stated that the "Central Agreement of the Army and Navy Air Forces for Operation" must follow the purpose of the previous agreement. A revision in strength was made and the plan for distribution was:

Central China Area

Army:

59th Air Regiment (20 fighter planes)

3d Air Brigade

    Headquarters of the 3d Air Brigade

    17th Independent Air Squadron (9 reconnaissance planes)

    18th Independent Air Squadron (9 reconnaissance planes)

    77th Air Regiment (24 fighter planes)

    45th Air Regiment (27 light bombers)

    75th Air Regiment (18 light bombers)

Navy:

2d Combined Air Unit (54 carrier fighter planes, 24 carrier attack planes, 12 carrier bombers and 26 land medium attack planes)

1st Combined Air Force (24 land medium attack planes)

3d Air Division (24 reconnaissance seaplanes)

South China Area

Army:

4th Air Brigade (13 reconnaissance planes, 24 fighter planes and 18 light bombers)

Navy:

1st Air Division (9 carrier fighter planes, 9 carrier bombers and 18 carrier attack planes)

14th Air Division (12 carrier fighter planes, 6 carrier bombers and 18 carrier attack planes)

Takao Air Unit (9 land medium attack planes)

One seaplane tender (8 reconnaissance seaplanes)

North China Area

Army:

Air Group

2d Squadron of the 10th Air Regiment (9 reconnaissance planes)

3d Squadron of the 64th Air Regiment (12 fighter planes)

27th Air Regiment (minus 1st squadron) (9 light bombers)

90th Air Regiment (18 light bombers)

1st Air Brigade

    16th Independent Air Squadron (9 reconnaissance planes)

    10th Independent Air Squadron (12 fighter planes)

    60th Air Regiment (45 heavy bombers)

Navy:

The Chingtao air unit (5 carrier attack planes)

In order to be ready to launch the second air attack operation at the required time, the Air Group commander ordered all units under his command to complete their training by early autumn.

On 1 September, however, the headquarters of the Air Group was transferred to Manchuria to assist in the final crucial phase of the Nomonhan Incident.[4] At the same time, Imperial General Headquarters ordered the organization of the 3d Air Group, the 3d Air Brigade and the 21st Independent Air Unit. The 27th and 98th Air Regiments from north China and the 45th and 77th Air Regiments from central China

---

4. Japanese Studies on Manchuria, Vols. IV and XI.

were transferred to Manchuria while the 4th Air Brigade Headquarters was transferred from south China to Formosa. In late September, the 11th and 59th Air Regiments were transferred from Manchuria to central China and placed under the command of the 3d Air Brigade commander.

Chart No. 5 shows the disposition of the air force in China in September 1939.

Imperial General Headquarters directed that offensive operations be continued in China and, at the same time, revised the Army-Navy Central Air Agreement as follows:

North China Area

Army:

3d Air Group Headquarters

    16th Independent Air Squadron (9 reconnaissance planes)

    60th Air Regiment (36 heavy bombers)

    2d Squadron of the 10th Air Regiment (9 reconnaissance planes)

    1st Air Brigade (9 reconnaissance planes, 12 fighters, and 18 light bombers)

Navy:

The Chingtao Air Unit (5 carrier attack planes)

Central China Area

Army:

3d Air Brigade Headquarters

Chart No. 5

Disposition of Air Force in China — September 1939

3d Air Group — Commander: Lt Gen Satoshi Kinoshita		
North China	Central China	South China
3d Air Group Headquarters 16th Independent Air Squadron (Headquarters' reconnaissance planes) 60th Air Regiment (Heavy bombers)	3d Air Brigade Headquarters 17th Independent Air Squadron (Headquarters' reconnaissance planes) 11th Air Regiment (Fighters) 44th Air Regiment (Reconnaissance planes) 59th Air Regiment (Fighters) 75th Air Regiment (Light bombers)	Unit Headquarters 82d Independent Air Squadron (Light bombers) 84th Independent Air Squadron (Fighters)
1st Air Brigade Headquarters 83d Independent Air Squadron (Reconnaissance planes) 10th Independent Air Squadron (Fighters) 90th Air Regiment (Light bombers)		
1st Air Brigade	3d Air Brigade	21st Independent Air Unit

79

17th Independent Air Squadron (9 reconnaissance planes)

44th Air Regiment (18 reconnaissance planes)

59th Air Regiment (24 fighters)

75th Air Regiment (18 light bombers)

Navy:

2d Combined Air Unit (33 carrier fighters, 6 carrier bombers, 6 carrier attack planes, and 27 land medium attack planes)

Air Unit attached to the 3d Fleet Headquarters (6 sea reconnaissance planes)

South China Area

Army:

21st Independent Air Unit Headquarters

82d Independent Air Squadron (9 reconnaissance planes)

84th Independent Air Squadron (12 fighters)

Navy:

3d Combined Air Unit (18 carrier fighters, six carrier bombers, 27 land medium attack planes, and 11 sea reconnaissance planes)

On 23 September 1939, Imperial General Headquarters published the order of battle of the China Expeditionary Army and, on 1 October, the Expeditionary Army assumed command of all Japanese forces in China.[5] At this time, the 1st and 3d Air Brigades, together with other units in China (with the exception of 21st Independent Air Unit

---

5. Monograph No. 179, *Central China Area Operations Record, 1937 - 1941*, Chart No. 3.

in south China) were placed under the command of the 3d Air Group commander.

The Commander in Chief of the China Expeditionary Army ordered the carrying out of offensive air operations to add pressure to and cause disturbance in the strategic and political centers of the enemy as well as to obstruct the reorganization of the enemy air forces.

The air units, under the command of the 3d Air Group commander, which were to participate in these operations were the 60th Air Regiment, a headquarters reconnaissance squadron (16th Independent Air Squadron) and three fighter squadrons (59th Air Regiment and 10th Independent Air Squadron.) The newly formed 60th Air Regiment which was to be placed mainly in charge of offensive operations, was engaged in intensified training at Nanyuan in north China, preparing for long-distance daylight attacks. It improved and strengthened its armament and occasionally cooperated with the ground forces. Early in October it moved to the advance base at Ani.

Progress of Operations

Although this operation called for the bombing of important areas in Szechwan Province, particularly important military establishments and enemy airfields, taking into consideration Japan's adverse political situation and also the disappointing results of daylight raids, Imperial General Headquarters ordered air activities to be limited to Shensi and Honan Provinces. Accordingly, the 3d

Air Group commander ordered the 60th Air Regiment, in cooperation with the 1st Air Brigade, to carry out raids against Changan, Paochi, Loyang, Pingliang, Fushih, Ichuan, Lochuan, Nancheng and Chiahsien.[6]

Outline of Third Air Operation (10 Dec 1939 - 31 Dec 1939)

After the conclusion of the Second Air Operation the Army Air Force continued training for both daylight and night attacks.

In November, the Navy Air Force repeatedly attacked Chengtu and Lanchow (usually at night) but they found it difficult to locate the targets and correctly judge the results of the raids. The Navy then suggested a combined Army-Navy operation. In consequence, "Ta-Go" Operation was planned as a joint daylight attack against Lanchow late in December.

The strength of the bombing force for this operation was approximately 100 planes, consisting of about 36 Army "Type 97" heavy bombers of the 60th Air Regiment, 36 land medium type attack planes of the 1st Combined Naval Air Unit and 28 land medium type attack planes of the 2d Combined Naval Air Unit.

The combined Army-Navy Air Force raided enemy airfields in the Lanchow area and the city of Lanchow on 26, 27 and 28 October. It shot down 20 enemy planes and inflicted severe damage on important establishments in the city of Lanchow, but the enemy air force retreated and frustrated the Japanese Air Force efforts to destroy it.

---

6. Although it is stated that planes were shot down, airfields were damaged and military installations destroyed, exact details are not available.

Army and Navy personnel worked in very close harmony both during the preparations and the operation.

Summary of Naval Air Operations

During 1939, the Navy Air Force carried out offensive operations over various parts of China. It made four air raids on Kweiyang in January, four on Kweiyang and Lungchou in February, and four on Kunming and Mengtzu in April. In addition, it made thirteen raids against Chungking and two against Chengtu and Liangshan between May and October, one against Chengtu and two against Lanchow in November and three against Lanchow in December.

Summary of Other Operations

During the year, in both central and south China, the 3d Air Brigade and the 21st Independent Air Unit cooperated closely with land forces carrying on mopping-up operations. During the Nanning Operation[7] the already powerful 21st Independent Air Unit received reinforcements of a squadron of fighters from the 64th Air Regiment and a squadron of light bombers from the 31st Air Regiment and actively supported ground operations.

---

7. Monograph No. 180, South China Area Operations Record, 1937 - 1941, Chapter 2.

CHAPTER 4

Air Operations in China

1940

Summary of Tactical Command of Air Operations in the Spring of 1940
General Situation and Disposition of 3d Air Group

In February 1940, intelligence reports were received stating that enemy aircraft planned to attack Nanching and Shanghai in an effort to disrupt the establishment of the new Japanese-sponsored central government. In order to confirm this, the Japanese Air Force reconnoitered the enemy's advance airfields in Chihkiang, Hengyang, Chian, and Kanhsien. Simultaneously, the air defense of Nanching and Shanghai was strengthened. Also in February, during the operation south of the Chientang Chiang, the Japanese Air Force attacked Chinhua, Yushan and Chuhsien airfields in order to counter enemy air attacks.

In March, there were indications that the Chinese Air Force would again become active and, in order to prevent this, between 30 March and 12 April, the Japanese Air Force raided Chian, Yushan, Shangjao and Yingtanchen.

Prior to this, the 3d Air Group had transferred its headquarters to Nanching and assumed responsibility for the direction of all phases of air operations over north and central China. The disposition of the Group on March 1940 was as shown on Chart No. 6.

Chart No. 6

March 1940

Disposition of 3d Air Group

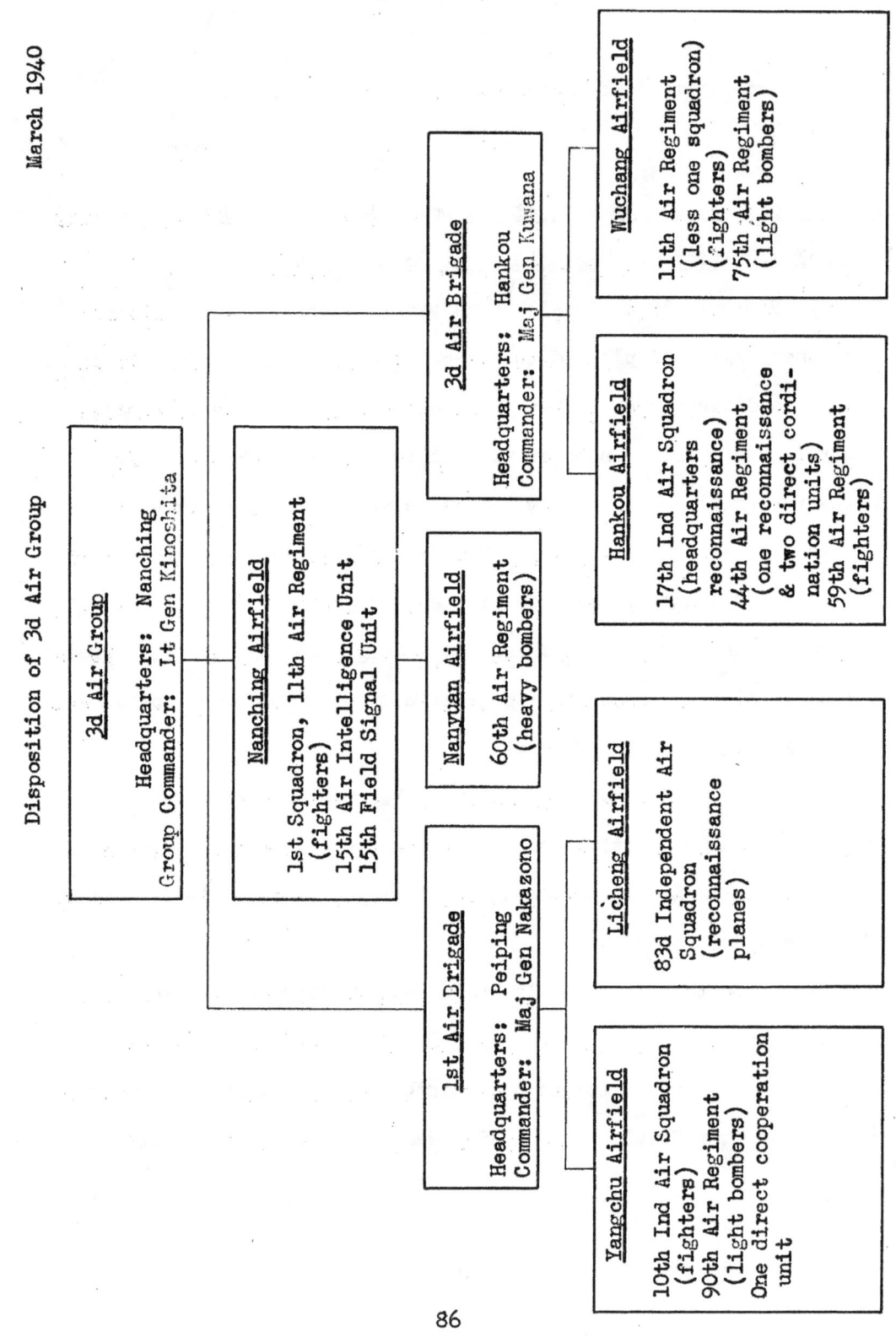

The mission of the 3d Air Group at that time was to suppress the enemy air force and to cooperate with land operations. The Air Group commander directed the 1st Air Brigade to cooperate with the land operations of the North China Area Army and the 3d Air Brigade with the land operations of the Eleventh and Thirteenth Armies. At the same time, the 60th Air Regiment, which was training at Nanyuan for coming air offensives, was attached directly to the Air Group commander.

Air Operations During the Ichang Operation

Past experience had proven the danger of unescorted daylight bombing missions in areas where enemy fighters were located. Realizing the necessity for providing fighter cover, the China Expeditionary Army planned to acquire an air base for Type Zero Navy fighters west of the Wu-Han sector. (The short-range, Type 97 Army fighters were not suitable as escort fighters for the planned Chungking Operation, even from Ichang.)

As the 3d Air Group had been ordered to support the Ichang Operation,[1] it, in turn, delegated this responsibility to the 3d Air Brigade, stationed at Hankou. At the same time, it transferred the 60th Air Regiment, a squadron of the 90th Air Regiment and a force of direct cooperation units to the vicinity of Hankou, when all units,

---

1. Monograph No. 179, Central China Area Operations Record, 1937 - 1941, Chapter 4.

with the exception of the 60th Air Regiment, were placed under the command of the 3d Air Brigade commander. The 60th Air Regiment remained under the direct command of the 3d Air Group commander. The 3d Air Brigade was directed to support the ground operations of the Eleventh Army and the 60th Air Regiment was assigned the mission of bombing strategic points to the rear of the enemy.

Direction of Air Operations in China by Imperial General Headquarters

In order to crush the enemy's resistance, in May, Imperial General Headquarters issued the Army-Navy Central Agreement, which, because of the situation in Japan and abroad, placed some restrictions on the bombing of non-military objectives.

Army-Navy Central Agreement Regarding Air Operations

15 May 1940

Operational Policy:

In China the Army and Navy Air Forces will cooperate to destroy the enemy air forces at an opportune time. They will attack and destroy strategic and political objectives and support sea and land operations in order to crush the enemy's resistance.

Army and Navy Air Forces will be concentrated and used wherever and whenever required.

Forces to be Employed:

Forces to be used are listed below. However, these may be transferred or their strength changed in accordance with the military situation.

a. North China

    Army: 1st Air Brigade (18 reconnaissance planes, 12 fighters, and 18 light bombers).

    60th Air Regiment (36 heavy bombers).

    3d Squadron of the 15th Air Regiment (9 reconnaissance planes).

    Navy: Chingtao Air Unit (6 carrier attack planes and 2 reconnaissance seaplanes).

b. Central China

    Army: 3d Air Group Headquarters.

    3d Air Brigade (27 reconnaissance planes, 24 fighters and 18 light bombers).

    11th Air Regiment (27 fighters).

    Navy: 2d Combined Air Unit.

    12th Air Division (27 carrier-fighter planes, 9 carrier attack planes, and 9 carrier bombers).

    13th Air Division (27 land medium attack planes and 6 land reconnaissance planes).

    River Base Flying Unit (6 reconnaissance seaplanes).

c. South China

    Army: 21st Independent Air Unit (9 reconnaissance planes and 12 fighters).

    One squadron of the 64th Air Regiment (12 fighters).

    One squadron of the 31st Air Regiment (9 light bombers).

Navy: 3d Combined Air Unit

    14th Air Division (27 carrier-fighter planes and 9 carrier bombers).

    15th Air Division (27 land medium attack planes and 6 land reconnaissance planes).

    "Kamikawa Maru" (seaplane tender) (9 reconnaissance seaplanes)

    "Chokai" (Heavy cruiser) (4 reconnaissance seaplanes).

    Hainan Island Base Unit (3 reconnaissance seaplanes).

Outline of Operations:

a. General Air Operations

    The Army Air Force will be used chiefly in north and central China and the Navy Air Force will be used chiefly in central and south China.

    Whenever necessary, the air strength of the Army or Navy may be reinforced from each other.

    The division of China will be set generally as follows:

    North China: Shantung, Honan, Shensi, Kansu Provinces and the provinces to the north.

    South China: Fukien, Kwangtung, Kwangsi and Yunnan.

    Central China: Those provinces between those mentioned above.

b. Direct Cooperation with Land and Sea Operations.

    The Army Air Force will, in general, support

Army operations and the Navy Air Force, Navy operations. When the situation demands, however, they will assist one another.

c. Army and Navy Air Forces which are stationed in the same district or operate in the same air districts will cooperate in order to obtain the best results. Details, including the division of duty between the Army and Navy Air Forces of the district, practical methods of cooperation, arrangement and use of air bases and exchange of information will be decided upon by mutual agreement of the local commanders of the Army and Navy Air Forces.

d. In carrying out air operations, every precaution will be taken to avert the occurrence of any unnecessary dispute with a third country. Attacks on the following are strictly forbidden:

Cities and towns which are not used for military purposes by the enemy. Also cities and towns used for military purposes but where raids might possibly damage the interests of a third country.

Attacks on ships in waters where a ship of a third country is present.

Attacks on trains and stations on the Indo-China - Yunnan railway in the district in which France is interested.

Outline of Fourth Air Operation (29 Apr 1940 - 10 Sep 1940)

From the middle of May the Navy Air Force conducted successive attacks on Chungking and Chengtu. In the meantime, the Army Air Force had been busy preparing to attack the plains of Szechwan Province from north China in cooperation with the Navy's attacks from central China. This was known as Operation 100.

On 6 June, the Army units attacked Chungking. Later in the

month, they launched seven more attacks against Chungking. In the same month, they also attacked Liangshan twice; in July, Chungking, Chengtu, Nanchwan, Tungliang and Pishan each once, and in August, Chungking twice. These attacks, which inflicted considerable damage on the enemy, were suspended when the Air Force was called upon to support the troops occupying French Indo-China.

The Army air units participating in these attacks were under the direct command of the 3d Air Group commander, whose headquarters was at Ani. Using Ani airfield as a base, 36 heavy bombers of the 60th Air Regiment were used in the attacks while six headquarters reconnaissance and nine fighter planes belonging to the 16th and 10th Independent Air Squadrons respectively were charged with reconnaissance duty, escort duty and air defense over the air base.

The Navy Air Force attacked Chungking eight times, Chengtu twice and Liangshan twice in May, Chungking eleven times and Suining once in June, Chungking four times and other cities four times in July and Chungking eight times, Tzeliutsing once, Luhsien twice and other cities five times in August. The 17th Independent Air Squadron at Hankou was used for reconnaissance while 80 to 90 medium land attack planes were used for each attack. These attacks, in close cooperation with the Army Air Force attacks were very successful in damaging towns and inflicting casualties on the enemy.

The Navy Air Force units which participated were:

2d Combined Air Group

> 12th Air Division (27 fighter planes, nine ship-borne attack planes, and nine ship-borne bombers)
>
> 13th Air Division (27 land medium attack planes and four land reconnaissance planes)

3d Combined Air Group

> A detachment of the 14th Air Division (9 fighter planes)
>
> 15th Air Division (27 land medium attack planes and two land reconnaissance planes)
>
> Kanoya Air Unit (18 land medium attack planes)
>
> Takao Air Unit (18 land medium attack planes)

This operation, carried out over a four-month period by the main strength of the Army and Navy Air Forces, with Chungking and Chengtu as the main objectives, was regarded as the climax of a series of air operations in China as it not only destroyed military objectives but also greatly affected the morale of the enemy.

Outline of Air Operations During the Occupation of French Indo-China

When, on 5 September, Imperial General Headquarters ordered the commander of the South China Area Army to dispatch part of his army to occupy the northern part of French Indo-China, the 1st Air Brigade Headquarters, the 59th Air Regiment (fighter planes), the 90th Air Regiment (light bombers) and some ground service units already located in south China began preparations for the operations. On 14 September, further air units including the 3d Air Group Headquarters, 18th Independent Air Squadron (Headquarters' reconnaissance planes) 60th Air Regiment (heavy bombers) and other ground service units were dispatched to the area.

Since the occupation of northern French Indo-China was carried out peacefully, except for minor incidents, on 19 November, the 3d Air Group Headquarters, 1st Air Brigade Headquarters, 59th Air Regiment and 60th Air Regiment returned to their previous stations.

CHAPTER 5

Air Operations in China

1941

Outline of Air Operations During the Eastern Chekiang Operation

In order to cooperate with the Thirteenth Army's operation in eastern Chekiang Province[1] in February 1941, the 3d Air Group concentrated its main force along the lower reaches of the Yangtze River with the Air Group Command Post and the 1st Air Brigade (Headquarters, 90th Air Regiment and 10th Independent Air Squadron) at Tachangchen and the 3d Air Brigade (Headquarters, 44th Air Regiment, 59th Air Regiment and 75th Air Regiment) at Hangchou.

In April, the 1st Air Brigade cooperated directly with the 5th Division both during its landing operation and in the operations which followed, while in March and April the 3d Air Brigade supported the 22d Division in its offensive along the Chekiang-Kiangsi railway, and the 60th Air Regiment attacked important areas in the vicinity of the railway.

The 4th Air Brigade (8th Air Regiment and 14th Air Regiment) which had previously supported the South China Area Army in the landings in the vicinity of Fuchou,[2] on 9 May was placed under the

---

1. Monograph No. 70, China Area Operations Record, Vol 1 (Cutting Supply Routes in Central China.)

2. Monograph No. 180, South China Area Operations Record, 1937 - 1941, Chapter 4.

95

command of the commander of the 3d Air Group. It was stationed at Tachangchen and Hangchou and, together with the 75th Air Regiment, ordered to cooperated with the future operations of the Thirteenth Army.

Later, the 4th Air Brigade commander ordered the 75th Air Regiment to cooperate directly with land operations and the 8th and 14th Air Regiments to carry out attacks against important enemy areas to the rear.

About this time the main strength of the 3d Air Group was transferred to North China and ordered to assist in the Chungyuan Operation.[3]

Outline of Air Operations During the Chungyuan Operation

In order to support the North China Area Army's Chungyuan Operation (7 May - 15 June 1941), on 10 April Imperial General Headquarters ordered the Kwantung Army to place its 32d (light bomber) and 83d (reconnaissance) Air Regiments under the command of the China Expeditionary Army commander for the duration of the operation. The units arrived in the area on 19 April and were placed under the command of the 3d Air Brigade at Hsinhsiang airfield. The China Expeditionary Army then instructed the 3d Air Group, which had been supporting the Eastern Chekiang Province Operation with its main strength

---

3. Monograph No. 178, <u>North China Area Operations Record, 1937 - 1941</u>, Chapter 5.

deployed at Ani and Hsinhsiang airfields to cooperate with the ground forces of the North China Area Army during this operation.

The 1st Air Brigade (1st Air Brigade Headquarters, 90th Air Regiment (light bombers), 10th Independent Air Squadron (fighters) and one reconnaissance squadron of the 15th Air Regiment) at Ani airfield successfully supported the ground operations of the First Army, while the 3d Air Brigade (3d Air Brigade Headquarters, 44th Air Regiment (reconnaissance and direct support), 32d Air Regiment (light bombers) and the 83d Air Regiment (reconnaissance)) supported the operations of the 21st and 35th Divisions with equal success.

On 23 July 1941, Imperial General Headquarters published Army Department Order No. 517 directing the commanders of the China Expeditionary Army, Kwantung Army and the 1st Air Group (located in Japan with units in Formosa) to assist one another by transferring small air units to the areas where they were most needed at a particular time either in Manchuria or China. Until the war's end, this order was used many times as authority to move small air units from place to place according to the urgency of the situation.

Outline of Fifth Air Operation

With the successful conclusion of the Chungyuan Operation, the Fifth Air Operation (also known as Operation No. 102) was launched at the beginning of August. During this operation the 1st Air Brigade attacked Chungking, Tzeliutsing as well as important areas in north China using Ani airfield while the 3d Air Brigade attacked ships on the Yangtze River from Kingmen airfield and strategic areas in central China from bases at Hankou and Wuchang. The strength and disposition of the air forces used was: (Map No. 4)

1st Air Brigade:

    Air Brigade Headquarters

    16th Independent Air Squadron (Headquarters reconnaissance planes)

    90th Air Regiment (light bombers)

    12th Air Regiment (heavy bombers)

    98th Air Regiment (heavy bombers)[4]

    (Using Nos. 1 and 2 airfields at Ani)

3d Air Brigade:

    Air Brigade Headquarters (Hankou)

    17th Independent Air Squadron (Headquarters reconnaissance planes) (Kingmen)

    75th Air Regiment (light bombers) (Kingmen)

    44th Air Regiment (reconnaissance planes) (Wuchang)

    60th Air Regiment (heavy bombers) (Hankou)

Although the results obtained during this operation were regarded as satisfactory, on 12 September it was necessary to halt the operation in order to prepare for the Pacific Area Operations.

---

4. The 12th and 98th Air Regiments were transferred temporarily from the Kwantung Army for use in this operation.

MAP NO. 4

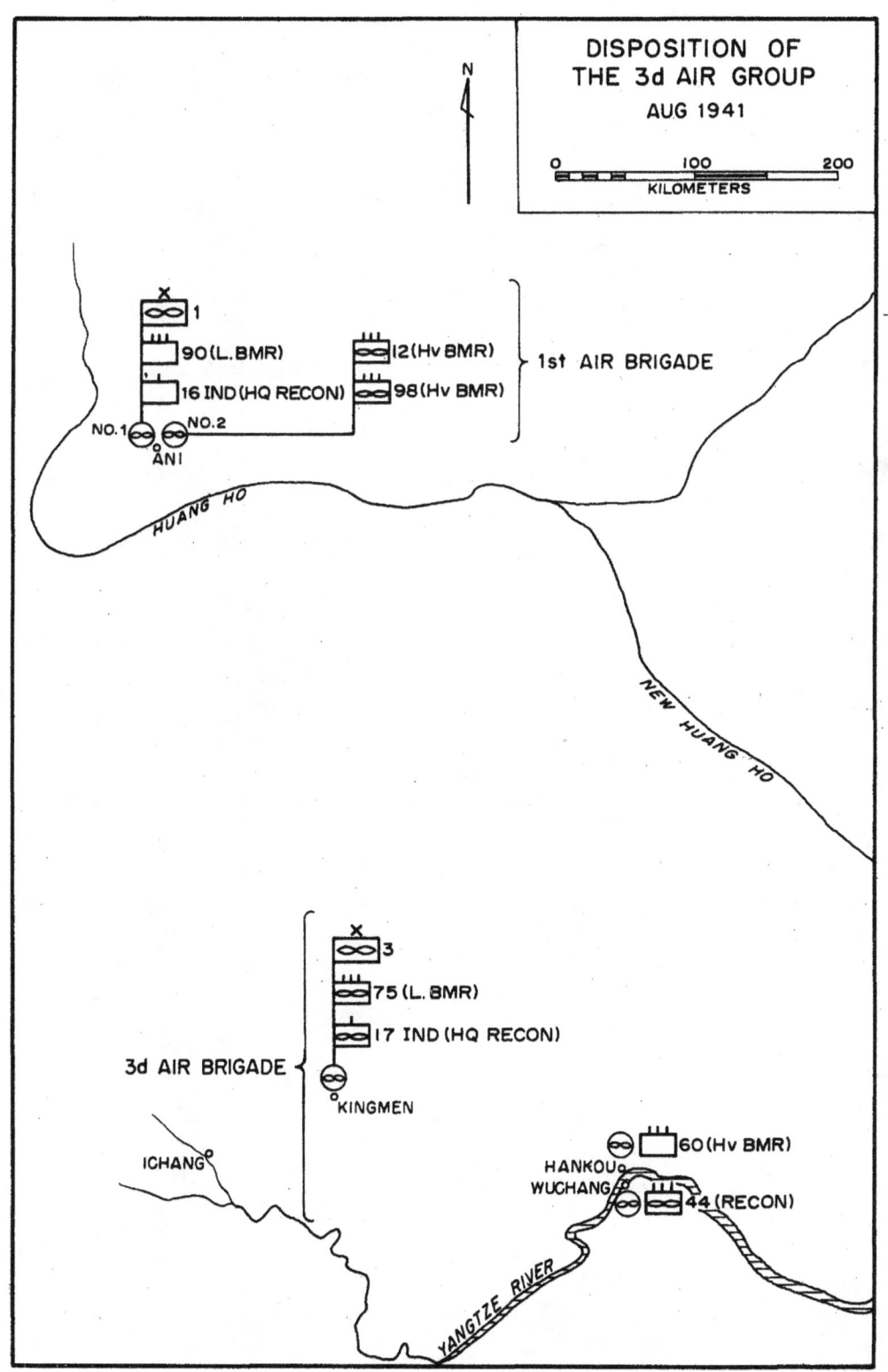

GENERAL REFERENCE MAP – CHAPTER 6
MAP NO. 5

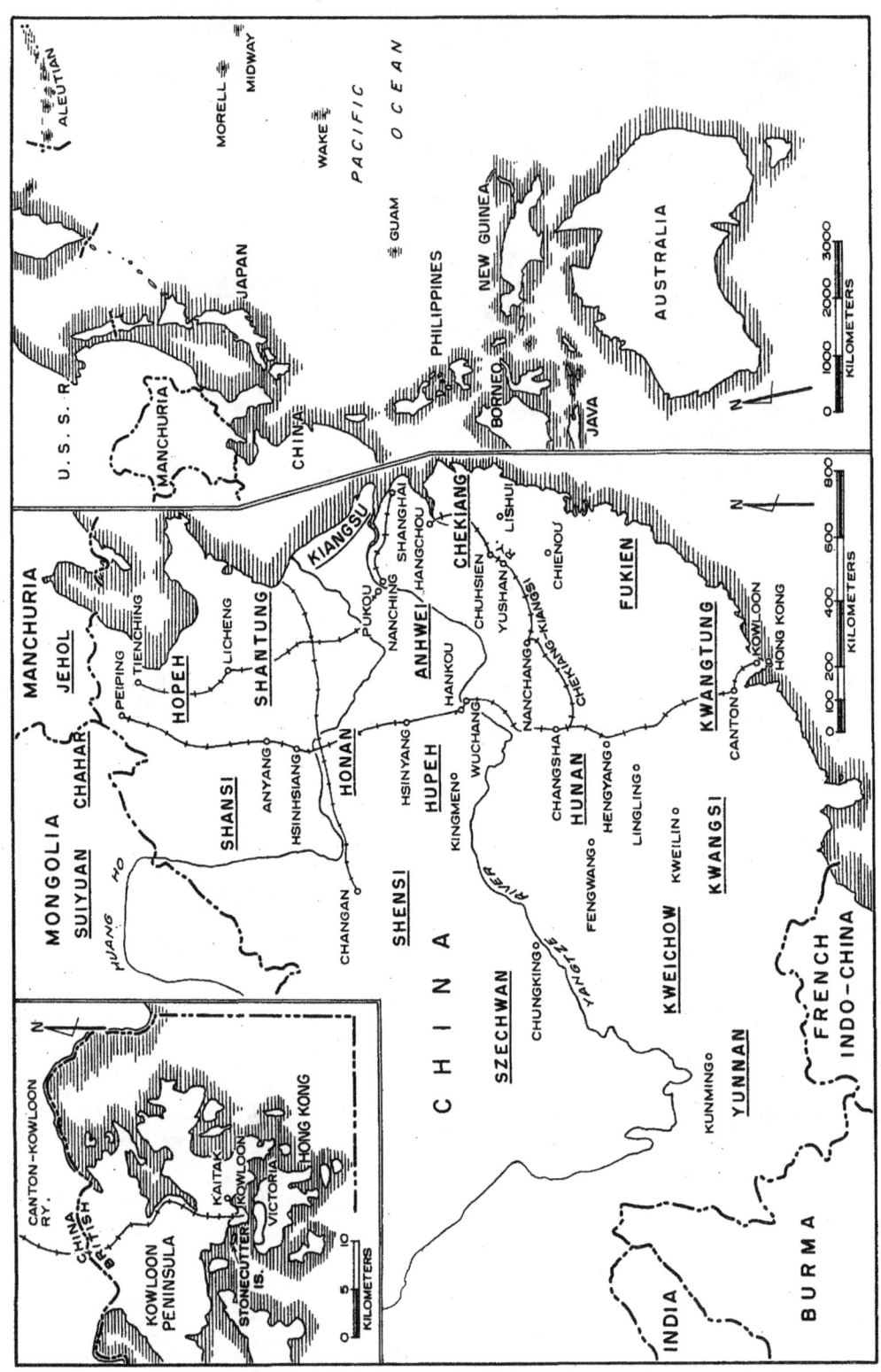

CHAPTER 6

Pacific War (Dec 41 - Dec 42)

Outline of Air Operations During the Hong Kong Operation[1]

In the fall of 1941, the 3d Air Group broke off its offensive operations against the interior of China in order to train and prepare its forces for the coming operations in the Southern Area. On 8 November, it ordered the 1st Air Brigade to prepare for the attack against Hong Kong. In December, the 3d Air Group moved south to Saigon and the 1st Air Brigade established its headquarters at Canton and began preparations as directed.

The air strength in China at the time of the Hong Kong Operation was:

1st Air Brigade Headquarters

    18th Independent Air Squadron (Headquarters reconnaissance planes)

    44th Air Regiment (One reconnaissance squadron and three direct cooperation air units)

    83d Independent Air Squadron (Reconnaissance planes)

    87th Independent Air Squadron (Reconnaissance planes)

    66th Independent Air Squadron (Direct cooperation planes)[2]

---

1. For detailed description of ground operations see Monograph No. 71, Army Operations in China, Dec 1941 - Dec 1943, Chapter 1.

2. The 66th and 87th Independent Air Squadrons are not shown in the China Expeditionary Army's strength for the Hong Kong Operation in Monograph No. 71. The reason for this is that as they were small air units. The Air Force records showed their location at a given time but Army records did not carry them. These were units that had been transferred in accordance with Army Order No. 517.

    8th Direct Cooperation Air Unit

    54th Air Regiment (Fighter planes)

    10th Independent Air Squadron (Fighter planes)

    45th Air Regiment (Light bombers)[3]

It was estimated that the British Air Force in Hong Kong at that time had only about ten planes.

Outline of Operational Progress

An air regiment (light bombers), together with one reconnaissance squadron, one fighter squadron and one airfield battalion, was ordered to cooperate directly with Twenty-third Army during the Hong Kong Operation. The Central Agreement between the Army and Navy, among other things, stated:

> At the outset of the operation, Army and Navy air units will attack Hong Kong. They will neutralize enemy air power and destroy enemy vessels in the harbor, as well as important military installations.
>
> *********************
>
> If the battle situation demands, part of the Army and Navy air units in action in other zones will be transferred to the Hong Kong Operation.

Despite the fact that the Army planes were long out-dated, the results they achieved were far beyond expectation.

In the early hours of the morning of 8 December, the Army air

---

3. Immediately after the conclusion of the Hong Kong Operation, the 45th Air Regiment was transferred to the Southern Area.

unit attacked Kaitak airfield and, by low strafing and bombing, destroyed all but two of the enemy's planes. On the 9th, in the face of heavy anti-aircraft fire, the air unit continued to attack key points around Hong Kong. On the 10th, the air unit bombed and hit two enemy gunboats off Hong Kong, partially disabling them. On the 11th, the unit directly cooperated with the 38th Division and greatly aided its attack against the main defense line on the Kowloon Peninsula. On the morning of the 12th, the main force of the air unit repeatedly attacked Stonecutter Island, blasting batteries and barracks and starting several fires. At the same time, part of the unit hit Kweilin airfield and destroyed two enemy planes that were attempting to attack the Japanese forces from the rear.

On 13 December, the air unit attacked and silenced the batteries on Stonecutter Island.

Encouraged by the unexpectedly rapid capture of Kowloon Peninsula, the Army decided to follow this up with an immediate attack against Hong Kong. It ordered the invasion troops to land and storm the whole island of Hong Kong. In relation to the air unit, the plan stated:

> **** The air unit and seige heavy artillery unit will support the movement of the landing troops by overcoming the fire of the enemy artillery and destroying the beach defense installations. ****

From 14 to 25 December, the air unit closely cooperated with the ground troops. On 16 December, a heavy bomber regiment (18 planes) of the 5th Air Group,[4] which had been ordered to support the attack against Hong Kong, bombed the battery on the west side of Hong Kong. In a series of attacks up to 25 December, the Army air unit bombed enemy batteries, positions and equipment and closely cooperated with the movement of the 38th Division. Further, it patrolled the sea and bombed enemy vessels. The air unit thus played a vital role in the capture of Hong Kong.

Outline of Air Operations During the 2d Changsha Operation[5]

With the outbreak of the Pacific War, the China Expeditionary Army approved the Eleventh Army commander's plan to assume the offensive in the zones south of the Yangtze River and ordered the 1st Air Brigade to support the Eleventh Army in this operation.

Throughout this operation the 1st Air Brigade gave very effective support to the land forces, especially during the capture of Changsha and later during the difficult withdrawal through strong enemy resistance. In the early phase of the operation the 44th Air Re-

---

4. The primary mission of the 5th Air Group, based on south Formosa, was to support the operation in northern Luzon Island. However, the full strength of the 5th Air Group was not required for this operation and one heavy bomber regiment assisted the 38th Division's attack on Hong Kong.

5. Details of the ground operations during the 2d Changsha Operation are given in Monograph No. 71, <u>Army Operations in China, Dec 1941 - Dec 1943</u>, Chapter 2.

giment (reconnaissance) made many sorties and, after 5 January, the entire Brigade participated in the operation and rendered invaluable assistance to the land forces.

Outline of Air Operations During the Chekiang-Kiangsi Operation

During early 1942, the enemy gradually strengthened its air forces in south China, especially around Hengyang and Kweilin. Also, aerial pictures taken by the 1st Air Brigade in late March showed that the runways on Chuhsien, Lishui and Yushan airfields had been increased from 700 meters to 1,500 meters; that ammunition and fuel were gradually being accumulated and that additional installations were being built. Furthermore, an airfield had been constructed at Chienou. This work was carried out under the protection of fighters that flew almost daily from Hengyang and Kweilin.

In early April, the 1st Air Brigade (using about 50 planes, including fighters and reconnaissance planes) attacked and destroyed a newly built enemy airfield in the Chekiang sector, destroying the runways and the majority of installations. Although the Brigade repeated these attacks again and again, each time the enemy succeeded in rebuilding the field.

Imperial General Headquarters, foreseeing that airfields in the Chekiang area could be used to advantage by the enemy as terminals in raids against Japan from air bases and carriers in the Pacific, as well as from other bases on continental China, ordered the China

Expeditionary Army to destroy enemy air bases in the Chekiang area.

On 16 April, Imperial General Headquarters drafted an operational plan, an extract from which read:

> Objective:
>
> The primary mission will be to defeat the enemy in the Chekiang area and to destroy the air bases from which the enemy might conduct aerial raids on the Japanese Homeland.

****

It further stated that the new enemy airfields and their attached installations were being skilfully camouflaged and decentralized and that they should be sought out and destroyed.

On 20 April, a further directive was issued stating:

> The Air Forces of the United States, Britain and China will seek bases in China from which to bomb Japan. They may also attempt to carry out air raids on Japan from Midway, Morell, the Aleutians and from aircraft carriers, in which event the logical terminal would be airfields in Chekiang Province.
>
> Air and ground units will be employed to capture and secure airfields in the vicinity of Lishui, Chuhsien and Yushan. Other airstrips in Chekiang Province will be neutralized by our air units at an opportune time.
>
> Consideration will be given as to whether certain air bases, together with the accompanying military installations and important lines of communication, will be destroyed completely or whether they will be occupied for a certain period of time.

In order to reinforce the 1st Air Brigade during its attacks against the airfields in Chekiang Province, in early April the Southern Army was directed to send the 62d Air Regiment (28 heavy bombers) and the 90th Air Regiment (20 light bombers) to central China.

On 30 April, Imperial General Headquarters ordered the Chekiang-Kiangsi Operation to be undertaken at the earliest possible date. The operation proceeded smoothly with the 1st Air Brigade cooperating with the ground units when required. Not only did the Brigade support the ground forces by bombing the opposing forces but its reconnaissance planes greatly assisted the operation by supplying information in regard to enemy ground movements, positions and strength.

Subsequent to the occupation of the captured areas, by mid-August units of the 13th Army had destroyed the Yushan, Chuhsien and Lishui airfields. The enemy, however, continued to reinforce their air force around Hengyang and Kweilin and, with the withdrawal of the Eleventh and Thirteenth Armies, it was feared that using airfields in Kiangsi and western Chekiang Provinces as staging areas, they would bomb the Homeland. The 1st Air Brigade, therefore, in spite of the fact that its fighting strength was gradually diminishing, repeatedly attacked and damaged airfields in this area.

At the beginning of August, the Japanese Air Force in China was disposed as follows:

Headquarters, 1st Air Brigade:	Hankou
18th Independent Air Squadron (Headquarters reconnaissance planes)	
Main force:	Hankou
3 planes :	Canton
44th Air Regiment (Direct Cooperation and Reconnaissance Unit)	Hangchou and Chuhsien
83d Independent Air Squadron (Reconnaissance planes)	Hangchou
8th Direct Cooperation Air Unit	Nanching
54th Air Regiment (Type 97 fighters)	
2 squadrons:	Hankou
1 squadron :	Nanchang
10th Independent Air Squadron (Type 1 fighters)[1]	Hankou
90th Air Regiment (light bombers)	
Main force:	Licheng
Element :	Peiping
24th Air Regiment (Type 1 fighters)[2]	Canton
206th Independent Air Unit (Direct Cooperation Air Unit)[2]	Peiping
Headquarters, 209th Independent Air Unit, together with 2 reconnaissance squadrons[2]	Nanchang

1. The Type 1 fighter was a new plane, superior in performance to the Type 97. This plane was known as the "Hayabusa".

2. These units were transferred from Manchuria to China on 1 July 1942.

  65th Air Regiment (Light bombers)[3]   Shanghai and
                             Hangchou

  62d Air Regiment (Heavy bombers)[4]

    Main force: Hsinyang
    Element :   Wuchang

Return of 3d Air Division to China

In order to strengthen the air force in China, Imperial General Headquarters ordered the return of the 3d Air Division Headquarters from Singapore. The Headquarters (which had been reorganized from the 3d Air Group on 10 June) arrived at Canton on 6 August and was again placed under the command of the Commander in Chief of the China Expeditionary Army.

Disposition of Air Forces under the Command of the 3d Air Division and Progress of Operations

While the 3d Air Division cooperated with the operations of the various ground forces in China, at the same time, in order to destroy the enemy air forces which had advanced to Hunan and Kwangsi Provinces, it disposed the air units as follows:

The commander of the 1st Air Brigade was ordered to advance to Canton and, using the main strength of the 18th Independent Squad-

---

  3. This regiment was transferred from Manchuria to central China on 4 May 1942.

  4. This regiment was scheduled to return to Japan in the near future.

ron, the 24th Air Regiment and the 10th Independent Air Squadron, to destroy the enemy advancing into Hunan and Kwangsi Provinces as soon as possible. Should this prove impossible, this force, using airfields in the Wu-Han area, was to conduct sneak attacks against Chungking.

The 44th Air Regiment (three Type 97 Headquarters reconnaissance planes and a squadron of the 54th Air Regiment attached) using Nanchang as its base, was charged with the responsibility of reporting the movements of the enemy at the main airfields in Kiangsi, Fukien and Chekiang Provinces and crushing the enemy's attempt to attack Japan from the air. It was also, at the appropriate time, to cooperate with the Eleventh Army's operations.

The 65th Air Regiment (83d Independent Squadron attached) using Hangchou as its base, was to cooperate immediately with the Thirteenth Army's operation while the 206th Independent Air Unit, from Yangchu, was to cooperate directly with the North China Area Army's operation. The 54th Air Regiment (minus one squadron) was responsible for the air defense of the Wu-Han sector.

The 90th Air Regiment was to continue night training at Peiping and Licheng while the 16th Air Regiment, upon its arrival in China from the Philippines, was to conduct night training exercises at Hsinhsiang and Anyang.

The 29th Independent Air Unit was scheduled to be returned to

Manchuria within a short time.[5]

About the end of August, the 55th Independent Squadron (Headquarters reconnaissance planes) and the 33d Air Regiment (fighters) arrived in China. The former unit was engaged in taking aerial pictures of the interior of China from its base at Kingmen, while the latter attacked the Kweilin - Liuchowhsien area from its base at Canton.

Toward the middle of September, the 65th Air Regiment which had suffered heavy casualties, was ordered back to Manchuria.

Although the 3d Air Division made every effort to fulfil its mission of destroying the enemy air force based at Kweilin, Hengyang and Lingling, the enemy refused to engage in a decisive battle.

Tactical Command of Imperial General Headquarters

On 10 December, Imperial General Headquarters notified the China Expeditionary Army that the future policy and conduct of operations in China was being carefully studied. Before defining the policy, however, grave consideration would have to be given to the situation of the Japanese Army in all theaters, as well as the shortage of shipping and war materiel. Aerial operations were to be carried out as

---

5. As there was no fighting in Manchuria at this time, units of the Second Air Army were successively transferred to China to support the operations there. When necessary, they were returned to Manchuria for replenishment of strength and further training, at which time they were replaced by fresh units.

the situation demanded and every effort was to be made to destroy the rapidly increasing enemy air forces. The conduct of future operations in China could not be planned in detail, however, until the successful completion of the first phase of operations in the Pacific.

Preparations were to be undertaken for air operations in China after the spring of 1943 when every effort was to be made to crush the enemy air force. In the meantime, air operations were to be conducted in accordance with the changes in the situation within their present boundaries.

The China Expeditionary Army was directed to carefully study the situation and to arrange for the use of Type 2 single seater fighters on at least one of each of the front line airfields in north, central and south China as promptly as possible.

GENERAL REFERENCE MAP – CHAPTER 7
MAP NO. 6

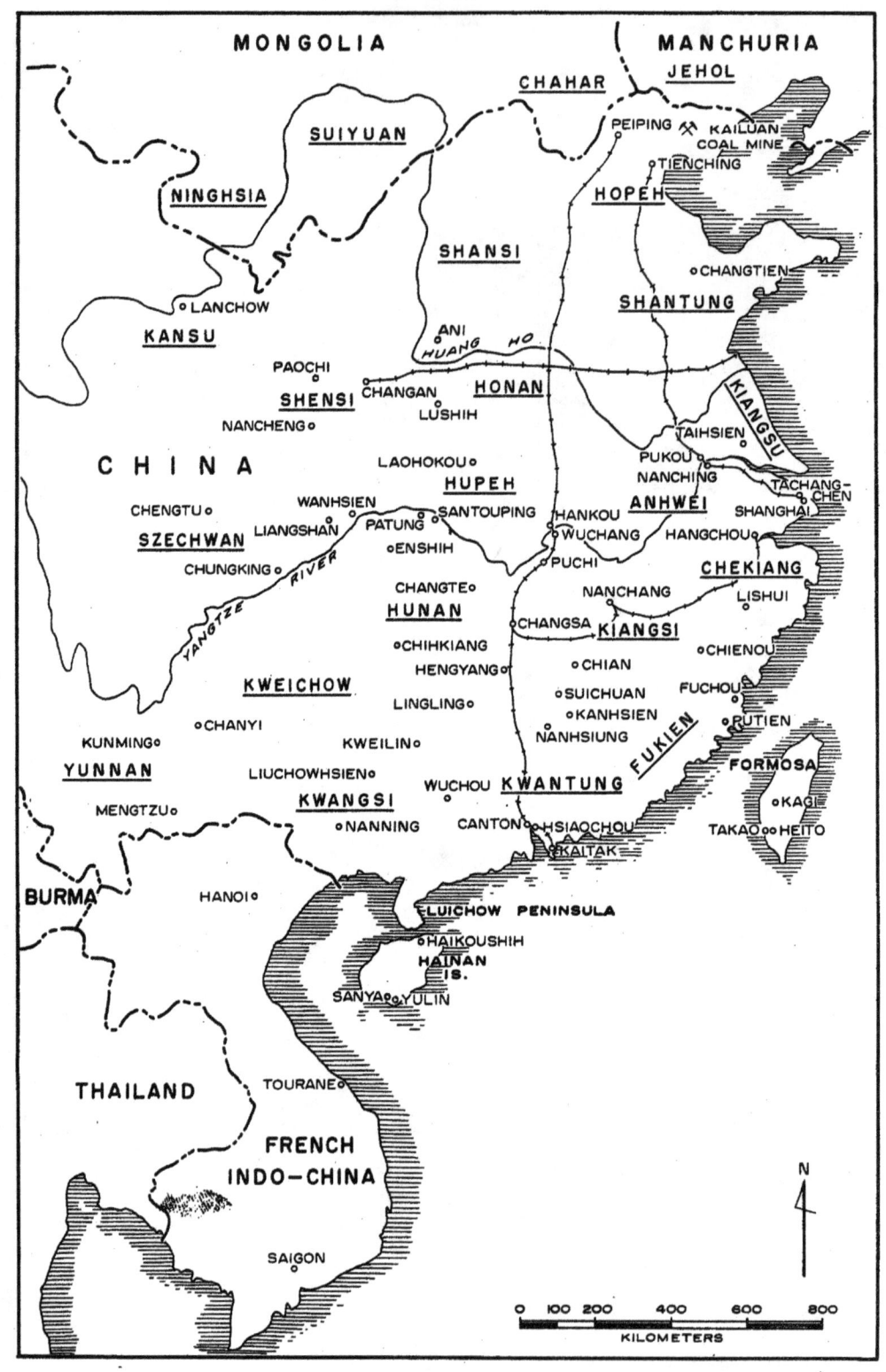

CHAPTER 7

Air Operations in China

1943

It was estimated that at the beginning of 1943 the United States Air Force had 44 fighters and 20 bombers and the Chinese 148 fighters and 43 bombers in China. The United States Air Force had assembled their main force at Yunnan and using staging areas in southwest China constantly carried out attacks against the Japanese forces in central and south China as well as in Burma.

It was believed that the enemy was building up its air force in Yunnan Province planning first to destroy the Japanese Air Force and lines of communication in China but with the ultimate objective of attacking the Homeland.

The Chinese Air Force appeared to be concentrated on Szechwan Plain and undergoing further training. When part of this force attacked the Japanese first-line bases they were found to be vastly inferior in equipment and in fighting spirit, however, it was a different matter when the well-trained United States Air Force with their superior planes joined the battles in the air.

Direction by Imperial General Headquarters in 1943

On 17 February 1943, Imperial General Headquarters issued the following directive to the China Expeditionary Army:

After the spring of 1943 the China Expeditionary Army will make every effort to strengthen its air operations. It will destroy the enemy's air strength and frustrate the plan to raid the Homeland from bases in China.

The aerial defense system will be equipped and strengthened in China. At the same time, every available means will be taken to carry out reconnaissance missions in order to report the exact situation of the enemy air force.

Necessary air reinforcements will be carried out after the spring of 1943. In the meantime, the Air Force will cooperate with the Southern Army in destroying the enemy air forces, particularly the United States Air Force, in the interior and southwestern sector of China.

Although it will depend on the situation at the time, it is presently planned to reinforce the Air Force in China with two fighter regiments and two heavy bomber regiments.

Air bases and navigational aids will be strengthened and completed in order to facilitate the operations of the air force and reduce the loss of planes.

Imperial General Headquarters gave serious consideration to a plan to launch an attack against enemy forces in Szechwan Province in order to strike a blow against the superior United States Air Force as well as to destroy the Chinese bases of resistance. It was felt that should this operation be successful, any attempt by the United States Air Force to raid Japan from bases in China would be frustrated. With the deteriorating situation in the Pacific, however, Imperial General Headquarters found it necessary to temporarily suspend this operation.

Progress of Air Operations in China

In mid-January, as it was the season for bad weather in southwest China, the 3d Air Division decided that it could conduct air operations more conveniently from the Wu-Han area and moved its main bases there. Between the latter part of January and mid-February, the 1st Air Brigade and other units were transferred from south China to the Wu-Han sector, while part of the 33d Air Regiment (12 "Type 1" fighter planes), part of the 55th Independent Air Squadron (Headquarters reconnaissance planes) and one Direct Cooperation Unit of the 44th Air Regiment remained in south China.

By the latter part of February, the 3d Air Division had established its headquarters at Nanching, and the 55th and 85th Independent Air Squadrons stationed there were placed under the direct control of the Division. The main force of the 1st Air Brigade (composed of the main forces of the 23d and 25th Air Regiments and elements of the 16th and 90th Air Regiments, together with the 18th Independent Air Squadron) was stationed at Hankou where it prepared for operations to destroy the Chungking Air Force, which had advanced to Liangshan, and the United States Air Force, which had advanced to southwest China.

At the same time, the Seto Unit (commanded by the commander of the 90th Air Regiment and composed of the main force of the 90th Air Regiment, one squadron of the 33d Air Regiment and one Direct Cooperation Unit) cooperated from Haikoushih with the Luichow Peninsula

Operation of the Twenty-third Army.[1]

The 44th Air Regiment, using Nanchang and Puchi as its bases, cooperated with the Eleventh Army's operation north of the Yangtze River.[2]

The 206th Independent Air Unit, based at Changtien in Shantung Province, cooperated with the operations of the North China Area Army.

The 8th Direct Cooperation Unit at Taihsien cooperated with the Thirteenth Army's operation.

From February until June, the 3d Air Division not only cooperated with the ground operations but also engaged enemy planes and bombed enemy airfields in an effort to deplete the enemy's air strength. The enemy, however, avoided decisive battles and its well organized intelligence system prevented the Japanese Air Force from carrying out surprise attacks. Its air strength was gradually increased making it daily more difficult to effectively bomb enemy air bases.

The enemy succeeded in strengthening its advance bases and constructed additional bases in southwest China. During the early part of May, the United States Air Force stationed units (consisting mainly of fighters) around Kweilin. From this time until the cessation

---

1. Monograph No. 71, *Army Operations in China, Dec 1941 - Dec 1943*, Chapter 4.

2. Ibid.

of hostilities, the China Expeditionary Army exerted its utmost efforts to reduce the threat from enemy air forces based in southwest China.

The following is an outline of the main operations carried out by the 3d Air Division from the beginning of 1943 until June:

The first attack on Kweilin airfield on 7 January was at 1103 hours. The 90th Air Regiment (16 light bombers) and the 33d Air Regiment (18 Type 1 fighters) attacked the runway of Kweilin airfield and other installations on the southwest side of the base. Fires broke out at two points. The second attack was launched at 1600 hours. The 90th Air Regiment (9 light bombers) and the 33d Air Regiment (9 Type 1 fighters) attacked the airfield and railway station at Hengyang. Due to a heavy mist the results of this attack could not be reported. At 1625 eight light bombers and seven fighter planes attacked the runway of Kweilin airfield as well as military installations in the city, causing many fires to break out.

In North China, the 16th Air Regiment (16 light bombers) and the 25th Air Regiment (11 Type 1 fighters), at 1220 hours, attacked and damaged the runway of Nancheng airfield and its attached installations.

During these attacks not a single enemy plane was sighted.

With the improvement in weather conditions throughout China, enemy planes showed signs of action. The 3d Air Division again took the initiative and, using Canton as its base, on 9 February, carried out the following attacks in south China:

At 1102 hours, the 90th Air Regiment (9 light bombers) and the 33d Air Regiment (7 Type 1 fighters) bombed and damaged the runways on Liuchowhsien airfield.

About 1100 hours, the 90th Air Regiment (8 light bombers) and the 33d Air Regiment (6 Type 1 fighters) attacked and damaged the runways and attached installations at Kweilin airfield.

At 1533 hours, the 90th Air Regiment (9 light bombers) and the 33d Air Regiment (3 Type 1 fighters) attacked hangars and the railway station at Liuchowhsien.

At 1603 hours, the 90th Air Regiment (2 light bombers) and the 33d Air Regiment (6 Type 1 fighters) attacked the Lingling airfield but were unable to contact any planes. The two regiments also attacked military installations in the city.

In north China, at 1137 hours on 9 February, the 16th Air Regiment (6 light bombers) and the main strength of the 25th Air Regiment, using Ani as a base, attacked the runways of Lushih airfield. At 1225 hours, six light bombers of the 16th Air Regiment attacked and severely damaged Laohokou air base.

During these operations, the Division was unable to locate any enemy planes.

On 11 February, the 90th Air Regiment (17 light bombers) and a squadron of the 33d Air Regiment (8 Type 1 fighters) attacked the air base at Kweilin at 1113 hours and at 1610. On the same day, 15 light bombers and three Type 1 fighters raided Liuchowhsien base. No enemy planes were sighted.

On 24 February, having received information that the enemy planes were using Liangshan airfield, the 25th Air Regiment (15 Type 1 fighters) and the 16th Air Regiment (12 light bombers) attacked this base and the surrounding area as well as Wanhsien pier. At this time they succeeded in engaging three enemy P-43 fighters, one of which was shot down.

It was known that since the middle of February the United States Air Force in China had been steadily preparing for its next operation. Intelligence reports stated that, on the afternoon of 31 March, they had advanced about 40 fighters and seven B-25's to Kweilin and Lingling and that they were demanding weather reports for 1 April for the coast of Fukien Province with Fuchou as the center showing clearly that they were planning not only attacks on the China front but also against the Homeland.

On 31 March, the 3d Air Division ordered a squadron of the 33d Air Regiment, using six Type 1 fighters, to attack Kweilin. A few enemy planes were sighted but they retreated before they could be engaged.

On 1 April, twelve planes of the 1st Air Brigade (4 Type 1 fighters from the 25th Air Regiment and six Type 1 fighters and two

Type 2 fighters from the 33d Air Regiment) advanced to Hengyang and Lingling and, about 0900 hours, engaged more than twenty P-40's over Lingling. Four enemy planes were shot down. The 1st Air Brigade lost four planes.

At 1300 hours on 1 April, the 44th Air Regiment, using nine reconnaissance planes under the protection of six fighter planes of the 25th Air Regiment, bombed and damaged the runway at Chienou air base.

On 1 April, in order to report any enemy attempt to bomb Japan, the 55th Independent Air Squadron using four Type 100 Headquarters reconnaissance planes formed a patrol line extending over 350 km down the coast of Fukien Province from Lishui to Putien. Further, having received information that the United States Air Force was constructing facilities at Lishui in preparation for air raids against Japan, the 83d Independent Air Squadron using approximately 80 reconnaissance planes continuously bombed Lishui and the surrounding area for three days from 30 March.

At 1444 hours on 24 April, 44 fighters of the 1st Air Brigade engaged 11 P-40's in combat over Lingling air base. Three enemy planes were shot down and one was destroyed on the ground. Japanese losses were one shot down and one lost while returning to its base.

On 29 April, twenty-three fighters and nine light bombers of the 1st Air Brigade flew over Lingling air base. No enemy planes were encountered in the air, but two small planes on the ground were damaged and military installations in the city were bombed.

There were definite signs that the United States Air Force was gradually building up its strength in the interior of China and, by 30 April, the total number of enemy planes at Hengyang and Lingling was estimated to be only about seven or eight fighters, three or four of which were being repaired, and several B-25's.

From 1410 on 4 May, however, six B-24's, under the protection of eleven fighters, made repeated attacks for about forty minutes on Sanya and Yuling on Hainan Island. It was believed that they used Mengtzu and Nanning as bases. This was the first time B-24's had been used since they had attacked the Kailuan coalmine in north China the previous winter.

On 6 May, the United States Air Force began to assemble its fighters at Kweilin and, by 8 May, had approximately 52 planes in the area. Also at this time, a further 15 fighters that had been advanced to Lingling were returned to Kweilin, making a total of approximately 67 planes on Kweilin field.

As it was the enemy's tactics to give their bombers powerful fighter protection, it was estimated that they were preparing to advance a bomber command to Kweilin. On 8 May, approximately ten B-25's with strong fighter protection bombed Canton city and airfield, inflicting slight damage in both areas.

Poor weather prevented the 3d Air Division from carrying out its plan of destroying enemy planes.

On 14 May, it was learned that fourteen enemy fighters had moved from Yunnan to Lingling and the location and number of enemy planes on that day was believed to be:

Lingling:	P-40	13
Kweilin:	P-38	1
	P-40	11
	P-43	1
	B-25	3
	B-24	8

Meanwhile, a part of the Chungking Air Force, cooperating with the United States Air Force, advanced to Liangshan and attacked the Wu-Han sector.

At 1500 hours on 6 June, the 1st Air Brigade, using the main strength of the 33d Air Regiment (14 Type 1 fighters) and one squadron of the 90th Air Regiment (8 light bombers), made a successful surprise attack on Liangshan. It burned about twenty small planes as well as a number of gasoline supply cars.

At 1525 hours on the 10th, 16 light bombers of the 90th Air Regiment, 8 Type 1 fighters of the 25th Air Regiment and 19 Type 1 fighters of the 33d Air Regiment attacked the air base at Hengyang and bombed five enemy planes on the ground. This force also engaged about ten P-40's in the air, shooting down and destroying five of them.

Although the 3d Air Division spread its small strength over a wide front and exerted every effort to destroy the enemy's planes and prevent their advance eastward, the United States Air Force succeeded in establishing strong bases in southwest China from which combined fighter and bomber units daily bombed the central and southern areas. The location of enemy air forces in late June was judged to be:

United States Air Force

Kweilin - Hengyang - Lingling District
- Fighters 26
- Bombers 23 (B-25's - 14, B-24's - 9)

Yunnan District
- Fighters 11
- Bombers 16 (B-24's)

Liangshan, Chungking, Chihkiang and Chanyi.
- Fighters 26

Chungking Air Force

Chungking District
- Fighters 35
- Bombers 8

Chengtu District
- Fighters 80
- Bombers 10

Lanchow and Yunnan

Fighters   11

Southern Army's Air Operations Against China

As it was considered absolutely essential that the United States air bases in Yunnan Province be destroyed Imperial General Headquarters directed the Japanese Air Force in Burma to cooperate with the force in China. On 15 May, the 5th Air Division of the Southern Army attacked Yunnan air base and destroyed eight large planes and severely damaged five others. It also shot down eight fighter planes and one transport plane.

Navy Air Operations

The Navy had a very small air force in China, composed of several fighter and training units stationed at Hainan (Sanya and Haikoushih) and Kaitak, used mainly for air defense.

Preparations for Air Operations During the Summer

In order to assist in checking enemy air activities in China, during the early part of 1943 Imperial General Headquarters directed the dispatch to this theater of the 85th Air Regiment (Type 2 single-engine fighters) from Manchuria in June and the 8th Air Brigade (Type 97 heavy bombers of the 58th and 60th Air Regiments) from the Southern Army by the end of September. Actually, these reinforcements reached China between 3 and 13 July when they were placed under the 3d Air Division. At that time the China Expeditionary Army informed the 3d Air Division that this was a temporary transfer and that the units from the Southern Army, would be returned to a place designated by the Southern Army to arrive there not later than 10 October. Further, that every effort would be made to see that personnel and equipment were replenished before the units were returned. In addition, grave consideration would be given to the seriousness of the situation and the results to be achieved before using heavy bombers. The 3d Air Division was also required to report whether it would be necessary to employ two air regiments continually until October or whether it would be possible to return one regiment sooner.

The 3d Air Division commander had already completed his plans to include the use of the reinforcements and as the deployment of ground units was completed about 10 July, he immediately dispatched the 8th Air Brigade Headquarters, together with the 60th and 85th Air Regiments to Nanching. The 58th Air Regiment was sent to Tachangchen to begin the necessary training. About 12 July, the headquarters of the Division moved its command post to Hankou.

3d Air Division's Summer Air Operations Plan

In planning its summer air operations, the 3d Air Division commander found it necessary to take into account the fact that the increase in strength was restricted by time. Careful consideration had to be given to its employment in order to obtain the best results within the time limit and, at the same time, to preserve its war potential. Although it was highly desirable to destroy the United States bases in Yunnan, this was not feasible as poor weather conditions combined with the fact that the bases in north French Indo-China were not adequate for long term employment by the main force of the Division would mean that very few attacks could be launched. It was decided, therefore, to focus attacks on the United States Air Force at Kweilin and its vicinity and to direct incessant attacks against the front line bases. Although it was recognized that the excellence of the enemy's intelligence would prevent surprise attacks, it was felt that every advantage should be taken of the increase in air strength. It was planned to take every advantage of the weather. Heavy bomber units were to attack Szechwan Province and threaten Chungking, while lightning attacks were to be made against enemy air bases in Yunnan Province. Every effort was to be expended to prevent the enemy from attacking the Homeland.

The important points of the 3d Air Division's summer operations plan were:

Policy of Operation:

While fierce and incessant air raids will be made against the United States air forces in southwest China from the Wu-Han sector, lightning attacks will be made on Chungking whenever possible. Later, the main force of the Division will advance toward Canton and French Indo-China to attack the enemy air forces in Yunnan Province. At all times, strict attention will be given to preventing the enemy from attacking Japan from the air.

Outline of Plan:

First Phase (end July to mid-August):

During the first phase, the enemy air force north of Kweilin will be continually attacked.

Second Phase (mid to end August):

The 3d Air Division will advance and attack Chungking. It will destroy the military establishments there and also attack and destroy vessels on the Yangtze River.

Third Phase (beginning to end September):

The main force of the Division will be dispatched to south China and French Indo-China and will attack Kweilin and bases in Yunnan Province.

During this operation there will be close liaison between the air forces in central and south China and French Indo-China. Chienou and Chian aerodromes, which are the enemy front line bases for attacks against the Homeland, will be kept under strict surveillance and the enemy will be prevented from using them.

An element of the Division will be assigned for air defense in important areas, such as along the Yangtze River.

Progress of Operation

First Phase: (23 July to 22 August)

By mid-July the 3d Air Division had completed its preparations for the operations and awaited an opportunity to attack the enemy.

Due to poor weather, however, it was unable to carry out attacks successfully. In spite of this, between 23 July and 22 August, the Division attacked Hengyang aerodrome nine times, Lingling three times, Kweilin twice (fighters only), Chienou nine times and Paochi and Chihkiang each twice. The results achieved were:

- P-40   49 planes (seven unconfirmed) shot down
- P-38   One plane shot down
- P-24   Two planes shot down

During this time, the enemy air force frequently attacked Hong Kong and Canton. It was estimated that eleven P-38's, nineteen to twenty-three P-40's and one P-43, as well as 35 pilots were transferred from Yunnan area to Kweilin and Lingling. Enemy fighters at Kweilin, Lingling, Hengyang and vicinity were estimated to be between 60 and 70 in the middle of August. Headquarters reconnaissance planes reported that there were seventeen B-24's, ten B-25's, six twin-engine planes and 34 small type planes on Yunnan airfields and 13 large planes and three small planes on Chanyi field.

<u>Second Phase</u> (22 August to 8 September):

Despite the positive action taken by the 3d Air Division, the United States Air Force continued to increase its strength in southwest China.

As poor weather prevented the Division from attacking the enemy territory, the Division decided to first carry out blitzkrieg attacks on Szechwan Plain and then switch the main force toward French Indo-China and south China and direct operations toward Yunnan Province and Kweilin from this area.

In preparations for operations from French Indo-China and south China, on 23 August the 25th Air Regiment (17 planes) the 33d Air Regiment (14 planes) and the 58th Air Regiment (21 planes) under the 8th Air Brigade commander attacked military establishments at Chungking. They also attacked Wanhsien and Chienou until 8 September. The main objectives and number of attacks were:

Chungking (military establishments)	Once
Wanhsien, Patung and Santouping (Vessels)	Three times
Chienou (aerodrome)	Three times
Wuchou (aerodrome)	Twice
Nanhsiung	Once

Planes shot down were:

P-40	11 planes (three unconfirmed)
P-43	5 planes (three unconfirmed)
B-24	6 planes
Unknown type	1 plane

Vessels:

Sunk	1000 ton class	3 ships
	500 ton class	1 ship
Damaged	1000 ton class	1 ship
	500 ton class	5 ships
	Tanker	1 ship

Third Phase (9 September to 7 October):

The 3d Air Division successfully advanced its bases to south China and French Indo-China and by early September had completed its preparations for attacks on Yunnan and Kweilin areas. During this time, Lt Gen Moritaka Nakazono, together with his staff officers in charge of operations and intelligence, flew from Kagi, Formosa to the command post at Canton. At 1745 hours on 9 September the plane in which General Nakazono was flying was shot down over Hsiaochou, 10 km southeast of Canton and the General was killed. The Commander in Chief of the China Expeditionary Army then ordered Maj Gen Rokuro Imanishi, commander of the 1st Air Brigade, to assume command of the Division until Lt Gen Takuma Shimoyama arrived at Canton a few days later.

The disposition of the 3d Air Division on 9 September was:

    3d Air Division Command Post - Canton

    8th Air Brigade

        8th Air Brigade Headquarters - Hanoi

        25th Air Regiment (main strength)
        (Type 1 fighters) - Hanoi

        33d Air Regiment (main strength)
        (Type 1 fighters) - Hanoi

        58th Air Regiment (Type 97 heavy bombers) - Saigon

        60th Air Regiment (Type 97 bombers) - Tourane

        18th Independent Air Squadron (Type 100 reconnaissance planes) - Tourane, Hanoi

1st Air Brigade

    1st Air Brigade Headquarters - Canton

    85th Air Regiment (Type 2 single-engine fighters) - Canton

    90th Air Regiment (Type 99 light bombers) - Kagi (Formosa)

    55th Independent Air Squadron (Type 100 reconnaissance planes) - Canton

Air-Defense Unit in key areas

Part of the 25th Air Regiment (Type 1 fighters) - Hankou and Nanching

Part of the 33d Air Regiment (Type 1 fighters) - Wuchang

Others

16th Air Regiment (Type 99 light bombers) - Being converted into Model 2 light bombers in Shanghai and in Japan

44th Air Regiment (reconnaissance and direct-cooperation planes) - Cooperating with ground troops in Hankou and Shanghai

The 206th Independent Air Unit (Direct Cooperation Planes):

    Cooperating with ground troops in north China as well as reporting on the activities of enemy submarines.

Five Training Air Units: Being trained in central and north China

On 7 September, Imperial General Headquarters directed the China Expeditionary Army to take the following action in regard to the employment of air units in China:

> Having regard to the over-all war situation, the 8th Air Brigade (including the 33d Air Regiment) will be transferred to the Southern Army in early October. The 85th Air Regiment will remain in China for the time being. During air operations in south China, the Japanese Army will be permitted to use Heito and Kagi air bases.

Although the 3d Air Division had planned to make a series of attacks against Yunnan Province, due to bad weather conditions at this time, they succeeded in making only one attack.

An outline of the operation carried out at this time was:

Main Objectives and Number of attacks:[3]

    Yunnan Air Depot: One attack

    Kweilin Air Depot: Two (one attack was a combined fighter-bomber attack)

    Suichuan Air Depot: Two

    Nanhsiung Air Depot: One

    Kanhsien, Nanning and Chian Air Depots: One each

    Ships in the vicinity of Patung

Planes shot down:

    P-40   35 (nine unconfirmed)

    P-38   2 (one unconfirmed)

    B-25   1 (unconfirmed)

---

3. The exact amount of damage is not recorded. However, the main objective was to damage the runways so as to delay, if not prevent, attacks on the Homeland.

It was reported that three B-24's were shot down and eight of a total of 24 large type planes on the ground were destroyed during the raid on Yunnan Province, but these reports were not confirmed.

Ships:

Sunk	3 ships (each about 500 tons)	
Damaged	2 ships (each about 1,000 tons)	
	2 ships (each about 200 tons)	
	a large number of small ships	

During its summer operations the 3d Air Division shot down or destroyed on the ground approximately 103 enemy fighters and 21 bombers. Japanese losses were 25 fighters and 15 bombers missing, seven fighters and one bomber destroyed, 19 officers and 94 soldiers killed, four officers and 13 soldiers missing and 15 men wounded.

From the beginning to the middle of September those units to be returned to the Southern Army, were returned.

On 8 October, the Air Division commander withdrew his command post from Canton and returned to central China.

Air Operations from October to December

At the beginning of October it was estimated that the enemy had about 100 light bombers stationed at Kweilin. They also had a unit on Suichuan airfield and were beginning to use Kanhsien and Nanhsiung as air bases. From these bases they carried out repeated attacks against the Japanese forces in central and south China. As they were also receiving reinforcements from India, it was felt that unless Japan could increase the strength of its air force in China, the Japanese Army in that theater would have difficulty in continuing the war.

With the enemy's rapid gains in the south Pacific and in Burma, it was recognized that the over-all strategy called for the strengthening of the air force in those areas. At the same time, in order to remove the threat from the Homeland, it was necessary that the air force suppress the growing United States Air Force in China. The China Expeditionary Army, therefore, continued to attempt to smash the United States Air Force in China. It also strengthened its air defense at strategic points and improved its facilities at air bases in order to check the advancing enemy air forces.

Air operations ordered to be carried out from October to the end of December were:

> Continue aggressive operations to destroy the United States Air Force in China, especially around Kweilin. Attack and destroy the enemy forces whenever they advance to the east of Kweilin. (This does not include Kweilin.)
>
> If circumstances permit, attack Yunnan Province and cooperate with the Southern Army in its Burma Operation.
>
> Depending upon the situation, make lightning attacks against the Chungking Air Force.
>
> Direct cooperation will be given the ground force by reconnaissance and direct cooperation units. An element of the fighter and bomber units

will cooperate with the Eleventh Army during the Changte Operation.[4]

In order to support the Navy, an element of the Army Air Force will guard against submarines off the coast of China and establish air defenses along the Yangtze River.

The establishment and completion of airfields will be accelerated, particularly the air defense installations on the main fields.

After the summer air operations, the 3d Air Division continued to attack enemy airfields, taking advantage of every favorable opportunity. It also endeavored to improve its fighting strength by reorganizing and training its units with special emphasis on night surprise attacks. In addition, in order to conduct strong yet flexible air operations in the future, the Division planned to strengthen and extend its navigation, communications and intelligence sections.

Before dawn on 10 December, 15 P-40's, one P-54 and three B-25's were shot down or burned on Hengyang airfield. At dusk on the same day, eight P-40's, one P-38 and two B-25's were destroyed on Lingling airfield. In addition, the next day 49 fighters and bombers of the 3d Air Division attacked and destroyed 11 of the 15 enemy planes on the ground on Lingling airfield.

This was the first occasion on which the small Japanese Air Force in China had severely damaged the powerful enemy air force.

---

4. Monograph No. 71, *Army Operations in China, Dec 1941 - Dec 1943*, Chapter 4.

It had skilfully taken advantage of the darkness and had operated throughout all areas in China.

It was estimated that the enemy air force in China in December was:[5]

United States Air Force:

    Fighters: Approximately 160 planes (approx. 100 planes in the Kweilin area)

    Bombers: Approximately 70 planes (approx. 20 bombers in the Kweilin area)

Chungking Air Force:

    Fighters: Approximately 150 planes

    Bombers: Approximately 20 planes
(about 20 fighters and some bombers advanced to Enshih and Liangshan.)

---

5. Monograph No. 72, <u>Army Operations in China, Jan 1944 - Aug 1945</u>, Chapter I, p. 13, states that at the beginning of 1944 there were 500 U.S. planes in China. This was an Army estimate of the total number of U.S. planes being used by both the U.S. Air Force and the Chinese Air Force just prior to Ichi-Go Operation. There was a big build-up in enemy air strength in China in early 1944.

GENERAL REFERENCE MAP – CHAPTERS 8, 9
MAP NO. 7

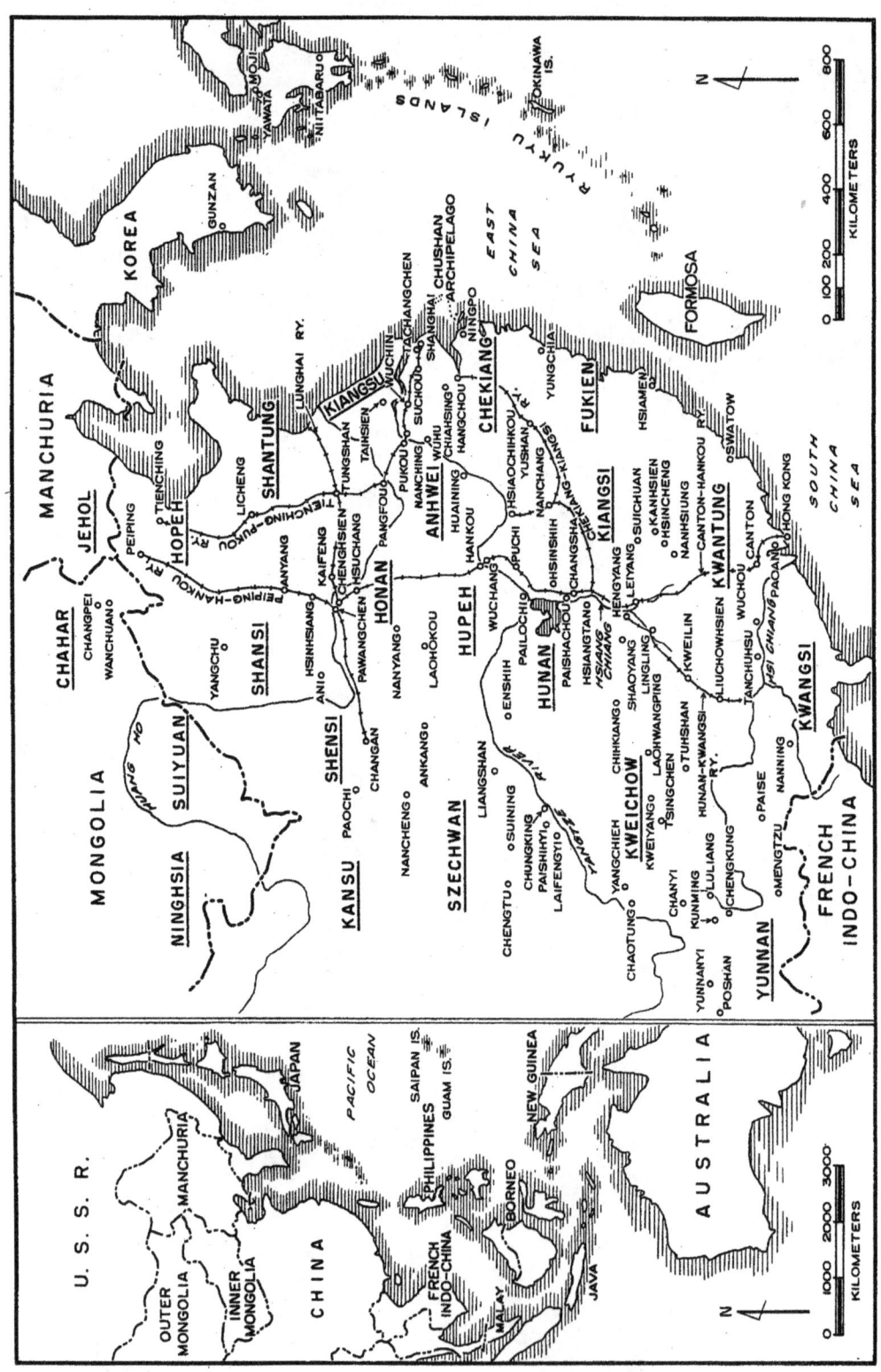

CHAPTER 8

Army Air Operations in China

1944

General Situation

In January 1944, Imperial General Headquarters approved the plan for Ichi-Go Operation[1] calling for the capture of strategic points along the Hunan-Kwangsi, Canton-Hankou and southern Peiping-Hankou railways, with the initial objective the destruction of Kweilin and Liuchowhsien airfields in order to alleviate the threat to Japan.

On 15 February, the 3d Air Division Headquarters was redesignated the Fifth Air Army Headquarters. The composition and disposition of the Air Force in China at that time was:

Fifth Air Army

Headquarters, Fifth Air Army	Nanching
1st Air Brigade	
Headquarters, 1st Air Brigade	Hankou
25th Air Regiment (Type 1 fighters)	Hankou
85th Air Regiment (Type 2 single-seater fighters)	Canton
16th Air Regiment (light bombers)	Anyang
90th Air Regiment (light bombers)	Tungshan and Canton
44th Air Regiment (Reconnaissance and direct cooperation planes)	Tachengchen

---

1. Monograph No. 72, <u>Army Operations in China, Jan 1944 - Aug 1945</u>, Chapter 1.

18th Independent Air Squadron (Type 100 reconnaissance planes)	Nanching
54th Independent Air Squadron (Direct cooperation planes)	Yangchu
55th Independent Air Squadron (Type 100 reconnaissance planes)	Hankou
105th Air Training Brigade (14th, 15th, 18th, 28th, 29th Air Tng Units)	Nanyuan[2]
Sector Unit, Signal Unit, Repair Unit and Supply Units	

It was estimated that the fighting strength of each unit (number of crew personnel and planes) was between one-third and one-half of the T/O strength.

About this time the 9th Air Regiment (fighters) was transferred to China from Manchuria.

The China Expeditionary Army planned to use part of the Fifth Air Army to support the North China Area Army during the Peiping-Hankou Operation commencing in the middle of April and the main force of the Air Force to cooperate with the Eleventh and Twenty-third Armies during the Hunan-Kwangsi Operation in the latter part of May. If required, support was also to be given to the Thirteenth Army's diversionary operation in the Yushan area.

---

2. Nanyuan airfield was located on the outskirts of Peiping.

Fifth Air Army's Plan

The Fifth Air Army planned to carry out operations against the enemy air forces in the area east of Kweilin until the rainy season in May and thereafter use its main force to cooperate directly with the Eleventh Army's operation.

The Type 99 light bombers, which were the nucleus of the bomber strength, were considered obsolete and of the three fighter regiments only one had Type 1 fighters whose range was comparatively long. Under these circumstances, in order to accomplish its mission, the Fifth Air Army drew up the following plan:

> Type 99 light bombers will assault and destroy enemy planes in night attacks on enemy airfields while the fighter units will shoot down enemy planes over the operational zone.

Estimate of Enemy Air Force Activities

It was estimated at the beginning of April that as a countermeasure against Ichi-Go Operation, enemy air activities were:

> To counter the Peiping-Hankou Operation, part of the enemy air force will attempt to destroy bridges on the Huang Ho, while at the same time cooperating with enemy ground activities. In addition, their main force is expected to continue disrupting transportation for the concentration of our forces.
>
> In the initial phase of this operation, the main strength of the Chinese Air Force is expected to participate using bases in Szechwan Province. Thereafter, part of the United States Air Force stationed in southeast China will join the battle. It is estimated that approximately 100 fighters and 20 bombers of the Chinese Air Force

and 60 fighters and 40 bombers of the United States Air Force will be used.

The enemy air force will establish bases in the Chungking-Chengtu and Enshih-Liangshan areas with advance bases at Nancheng, Paochi, Changan, Ankang, Laohokou and Nanyang. Intelligence reports state that the enemy is endeavoring to repair these advance bases and is massing fuel and ammunition at these points, but the work has not yet been completed. Some restraint, therefore, will be placed on the use of these fields.

During this operation, the main body of the United States Air Force, after establishing a base in southeast China, will strengthen its air power and advance its bases toward Fukien Province from where it will attempt to interrupt our transportation for the concentration of our forces. In particular, it will attack Japanese vessels on the Yangtze River and the China Sea.

During the Hunan-Kwangsi Operation, the enemy will attempt to disrupt transportation for the concentration of troops during the initial preparations for the operation. After the operation begins, they will try first to check the ground forces and cut our supply routes and then, by conducting repeated air attacks, to annihilate our air force. In the course of the operation their main air force will return to Szechwan and Yunnan Provinces for replenishment and will then return to attack the newly occupied areas.

It is believed that the United States Air Force, aided by the main body of the Chinese Air Force, will lead the attack. Judging from the present rapid rate of increase in reinforcements and the possibility of further planes being diverted from India, it is estimated that in the early phases of the operation enemy air strength will be approximately 500 United States planes and 250 Chinese planes. The present condition of enemy air bases in China would allow approximately another 300 planes to be diverted to this area.

During the operation the enemy air force will use its present bases in Szechwan Province and along the banks of the Yangtze River as well as establish new bases in southeast China. The enemy air force in Yunnan Province will primarily reinforce the Kweilin area while the air force around Yunnan and Chengtu will be gradually supplemented and strengthened from India.

As the operation progresses, the Eleventh Army will occupy Hengyang and the surrounding area but the enemy air force will continue its attacks from air bases at Chihkiang, Kweilin and Liuchowhsien. At this point, the air bases at Chihkiang and the area north of the Canton-Hankou railway will be situated on the flank of our advance. The enemy air force will undoubtedly take advantage of this situation to attack our supply lines.

Should the Eleventh Army succeed in occupying the Kweilin and Liuchowhsien areas, the main body of the enemy air force will retreat to the Kunming-Kweiyang and Chungking-Chengtu districts from which areas it is expected they will repeatedly attack the newly occupied zones. At that time, the bases in the Chihkiang district and advance bases at Tanchuhsu and Nanning must not be relinquished.

Although Ichi-Go Operation will hinder the enemy air force in its attempt to attack Japan or cut our communications and supply lines, judging by the manner in which their strength is being reinforced and their bases equipped, as well as their favorable situation in the Pacific, it appears certain that they will still endeavor to accomplish their mission. B-29's will be diverted to China in the near future when they will attack western Japan from this area as well as from bases in the north and central Pacific. It is probable that, upon receiving reinforcements, an element will move north to attack communication and supply routes and also our main bases of supply in north China and south Manchuria.

Situation Prior to the Operation (mid-February to mid-April 1944)

Enemy Situation:

It was estimated that by early March 1944 the United States Air Force in China had increased its strength to 340 planes of which approximately 160 fighters and 90 bombers were stationed in southeast China. This force frequently attacked vessels, harbors and airfields along the Yangtze River, particularly in the area around Hsiaochihkou, Huaining and Wuhu. They also attacked the occupied areas in north and south China and French Indo-China when weather conditions were favorable.

Fifth Air Army:

The fighting strength of the Fifth Air Army at this time was less than one-half its T/O stength. Although an average of 50 planes (mostly Type 1 fighters and light bombers) was being received each month from Japan, it was necessary to dispatch air crew personnel to Japan to fly them to China. This greatly hindered the training of crews.

The aviation fuel reserve was approximately 25,000 kiloliters (approximately 6,625,000 gallons) and about 3,000 kiloliters (approximately 795,000 gallons) were consumed monthly. Continuing at this rate, the reserve fuel would last only about six months. Therefore, about 10,000 kiloliters (approximately 2,650,000 gallons) of fuel were needed before August.

The bomb reserve amounted to about 7,500 tons of which about 200 tons were used monthly so that there was a two-year supply. However, the ammunition supply for 127 mm automatic cannon and 20 mm machine guns was low.

Peiping-Hankou Operation (mid-April - end May 1944)

The Peiping-Hankou Operation was launched on the night of 17 April.[3] On the 19th, Chenghsien was captured and, on 9 May, the Peiping-Hankou railway resumed operation. Meanwhile, the Fifth Air Army, in support of the land operations, conducted reconnaissance and bombing raids. The Air Army experienced great difficulty in protecting the Pawangcheng bridge across the Huang Ho. It stationed the 9th Air Regiment, composed of Type 2 single-seater fighter planes, at Hsinhsiang to provide aerial defense to this area. However, the regiment had only about ten planes which could be used and its advance warning radar at Kaifeng was out of order. It was impossible, therefore, to carry out interception operations successfully. Finally, on 29 April, 26 B-24's succeeded in bombing and temporarily damaging the bridge.

The strength of the various air units had been replenished by the middle of April and, most important, the 25th Air Regiment was up to full strength.[4]

---

3. Monograph No. 72, *Army Operations in China, Jan 1944 - Aug 1945*, Chapter 2.

4. Many of its pilots had become casualties during previous operations. These were replaced by new pilots from Japan.

In order to support the land operation, the Fifth Air Army stationed 10 Type 1 fighters of the 25th Air Regiment at Ani, 10 Type 2 fighters from the 9th Air Regiment, the 44th Air Regiment and the 54th Independent Air Squadron at Hsinhiang and about 20 light bombers of the 90th Air Regiment and the 16th Air Regiment at Anyang and ordered these units to cooperate with land operations. At the same time, it placed the bomber units under the command of the commander of the 44th Air Regiment.

On 29 April, the headquarters of the 2d Air Brigade arrived at Hsinhsiang, the main force of the 6th Air Regiment (Type 99 assault planes) at Anyang and the 48th Air Regiment (Type 1 fighters) at Nanching.[5] They were then placed under the command of the Fifth Air Army commander who, in turn, placed all air units in Honan Province under the command of the commander of the 2d Air Brigade. Meantime, the main force of the light bombers and fighters attacked important enemy airfields in Honan and Shensi Provinces and prevented the enemy from advancing in Honan Province.

The enemy had stationed a powerful element of the United States and Chungking Air Forces in the Liangshan-Enshih area and the main force of the United States Air Force in the Kweilin and Suichuan districts. Only a few P-40's conducted reconnaissance flights or attempted to intercept Japanese planes in Honan Province but the

---

5. These units were transferred from Manchuria where they had been under the command of the 2d Air Division.

main force frequently flew over central China and attempted to disrupt preparations for the Hunan-Kwangsi Operation. The Fifth Air Army commander, therefore, decided to attempt to secure air supremacy in Suichuan and Hengyang areas by attacking enemy airfields in that area before the opening of the Hunan-Kwangsi Operation.

On 6 May, approximately 45 enemy fighters and bombers carried out a daylight attack against the Wu-Han area, inflicting heavy damage.

Hunan-Kwangsi Operation (end May 1944 - Jan 1945)
To the Fall of Hengyang

Ground Operation:

On 27 May, the Eleventh Army opened the Hunan-Kwangsi Operation.[6] It assumed offensive after offensive and, in spite of continuous rain, on 18 June occupied Changsha and, on the 26th, Hengyang airfield. Due to the difficult terrain, shortage of supplies, insufficient concentration of heavy weapons as well as the superiority of the enemy air force, the occupation of the town of Hengyang was not achieved until 8 August.

With the development of the operation, the zone of occupation was reduced to a long narrow corridor along the Yangtze River and the Hsiang Chiang which was constantly subjected to enemy air attacks.

---

6. Monograph No. 72, <u>Army Operations in China, Jan 1944 - Aug 1945</u>, Chapter 3.

Because of the difficulty in repairing airfields and the delay in shipment of fuel and ammunition the Fifth Air Army was unable to advance its bases. In consequence, the fighter units which were charged with protecting the long lines of communication, were compelled to use Pailochi as their base. This meant they had to fly long distances to engage the enemy and so were limited in the number of flights made each day.

During this period the enemy air attacks against vessels, vehicles and railways were so severe that daytime transportation of supplies to the front became increasingly difficult.

Fifth Air Army:

On 18 May, the Fifth Air Army advanced its command post to Hankou and made the following general disposition of its units in order that it might cooperate to the best advantage with the ground operations:

The 1st Air Brigade (25th and 48th Air Regiments (Type 1 fighters)) was charged with the air defense of the Hunan-Kwangsi Operation zone, including strategic points; the protection of bomber units participating directly in this operation, and the protection of vessels on the upper reaches of the Yangtze River from Hsiaochihkou.

The Provisional Air Unit, composed of the 6th Air Regiment (minus one squadron) (Type 99 attack planes) and the 44th Air Regiment (minus an element but with the 54th Independent Air Squadron (reconnaissance and direct cooperation planes) attached) was to cooperation directly with the Eleventh Army.

The 2d Air Brigade, composed of the 85th Air Regiment (Type 2 single-engine fighters); a company of the 6th Air Regiment (Type 99 attack planes); a part of the 90th Air Regiment (light bombers); a part of the 44th Air Regiment (direct cooperation planes) and a part of the 18th Independent Air Squadron (Headquarters reconnaissance planes) was to give direct cooperation to the ground operation of the Twenty-third Army and aerial defense to strategic zones. After the completion of the Peiping-Hankou Operation, it was to conduct air battles in the Kweilin and Liuchowhsien areas.

The air units under the direct command of the Army, comprising the 16th Air Regiment (light bombers); the 90th Air Regiment (minus an element) (light bombers); the 18th Independent Air Squadron (minus an element) (Headquarters reconnaissance planes) and the 55th Independent Air Squadron (Headquarters reconnaissance planes) were to take part in the major air attacks during the Hunan-Kwangsi Operation, to destroy enemy airfields and to engage the enemy in air battles, whenever possible.

The strength of the force and the airfields used were as shown on Chart No. 7.

Chart No. 7

Fifth Air Army's Strength and Disposition — May 1944

	Strength	From the beginning of Operation to the Occupation of Changsha	From the Occupation of Changsha to the Occupation of Hengyang
1st Air Brigade	25th Air Regiment 48th Air Regiment	Pailochi	Pailochi
2d Air Brigade	85th Air Regiment Elements of 6th Air Regiment, 44th Air Regiment, 90th Air Regiment, 18th Independent Air Squadron	Canton	Canton
Provisional Air Units	Main Force of 6th Air Regiment 44th Air Regiment 54th Independent Air Squadron	Puchi (Pailochi)	Changsha (Pailochi) (Siangtan)
9th Air Regiment		Hsinhiang	Hsinhiang
16th Air Regiment		Anyang (Wuchang)	Anyang (Wuchang)
90th Air Regiment		Tungshan (Hankou)	Tungshan (Hankou)
18th Independent Air Squadron		Hankou	Hankou
55th Independent Air Squadron		Hankou	Hankou

( ) Indicates airfields used for staging.

The Fifth Air Army had made every endeavor to regain its fighting capacity and, by the beginning of this operation, had regained its power. The number of pilots at the end of May and their degree of ability is shown on Chart No. 8 (training units were omitted). In addition to the units shown on this chart, the 2d Air Brigade Headquarters, and the 6th, 9th and 48th Air Regiments were under the command of the Fifth Air Army.

The number of usable planes was:

9th Air Regiment:	11 Type 1 fighters
	14 Type 2 fighters
25th Air Regiment:	22 Type 1 fighters
48th Air Regiment:	26 Type 1 fighters
85th Air Regiment:	8 Type 1 fighters
	32 Type 2 fighters
16th Air Regiment:	19 Light bombers
90th Air Regiment:	20 Light bombers
6th Air Regiment:	18 Attack planes
44th Air Regiment:	11 Reconnaissance planes
	14 Direct Co-operation planes
54th Independent Air Squadron	2 Reconnaissance planes
	8 Direct Co-operation planes
18th Independent Air Squadron	7 Type 100 Headquarters' Reconnaissance planes

Chart No. 8

Actual Status of Pilots of the Fifth Air Army
as of 31 May 1944

Name of Units \ Classification	Officers					WO & NCO				
	Auth Strength	Assgd Strength				Auth Strength	Assgd Strength			
		A	B	C	Total		A	B	C	Total
Hq of the Fifth Air Army	1	1			1	5	2	1	1	4
Hq of the 1st Air Brigade	1	1			1	3	1			1
16th Air Regiment	12	8			8	36	14	2	13	29
25th Air Regiment	17	5	3		8	40	26	4	6	36
44th Air Regiment	8	8	4		12	26	14	5		19
85th Air Regiment	17	8			8	40	5	13	20	38
90th Air Regiment	12	8	1		9	36	9	3	12	24
18th Independent Air Squadron	4	6			6	6	11			11
54th Independent Air Squadron	4	3	1		4	12	9	1	1	11
55th Independent Air Squadron	4	2		3	5	6	5	1	2	8
15th Field Air Repair Depot	1	1			1	4	2			2
23d Field Air Repair Depot	1		1		1	1	2			2
24th Field Air Repair Depot	1					4	2	1		3
Total	83				64	219				188

The classification A, B, and C was an unofficial rating based on experience and number of hours flying time.

55th Independent Air Squadron   5 Type 100 Headquarters' Reconnaissance planes

Total

    Type 1 fighters   67

    Type 2 fighters   46

    Light bombers   39

    Attack planes   18

    Reconnaissance planes   13

    Direct Co-operation planes   22

    Headquarters' Reconnaissance planes   <u>12</u>

Grand total   217

With the opening of the Ichi-Go Operation, the number of pilots and planes gradually decreased and, in spite of every effort, it was found impossible to replace them, in consequence, the fighting capacity of the Air Army suffered. At the same time, as the 5th Air Army's fighting strength diminished, the enemy's air strength was rapidly being built up in China. A comparison in the number of planes is shown hereunder:

	End May 1944	Time of the Changsha Operation	Time of the Hengyang Operation	Time of the Kweilin Operation
US Air Force (US-Chinese air force) Chungking Air Force	520	600	750	800
Fifth Air Army	230	220	160	150

Remarks:
1. The number of enemy planes is estimated number of planes at the front, not including planes in reserve or used for training in the rear.
2. The number of Japanese planes includes usable planes only.

In order to strengthen the air bases in the Wu-Han and Pailochi areas, construction was begun on a second field at Hankou, two new fields at Wuchang and two at Pailochi before the beginning of Ichi-Go Operation. These fields, however, were not completed in time to be used during the operation. Operations were begun in the Hunan-Kwangsi area using Pailochi as the principal field and the fields in the Wu-Han area as rear air bases. With the development of the situation, bases were established at Hsinshih, Paishachou, Changsha and Hsiangtan. The bases at Hsinshih and Paishachou were used only temporarily while those at Changsha and Hsiangtan were constructed or restored as permanent airfields. Although the bases were poorly supplied with construction tools and supplies, the men made extraordinary efforts to prepare the bases and this, combined with the ingenuity of the air units, made it possible to conceal a few planes on each airfield. The narrowness of the occupied area, together with insufficient equipment and poor intelligence facilities, made it impossible to advance the greater part of the fighter units to the forward bases. The 1st Air Brigade, therefore, used Pailochi as the base of operations. When the focus of battle moved to the Hengyang area the fighters found it difficult to advance within striking distance of the battlefield. This permitted the enemy air force to move freely.

Outline of Air Operation:

During the Ichi-Go Operation, the main mission of the Fifth Air Army was cooperation with the ground forces. At times, however, it was compelled to engage the enemy air force in the air and to raid enemy air bases at night.

The Fifth Air Army sustained heavy losses during this operation and received little replenishment. It was compelled, therefore, to avoid air combat with the superior enemy air force whenever possible.

Toward the end of May the 1st Air Brigade advanced to Pailochi. When the Eleventh Army opened its attack, the 1st Air Brigade patrolled key areas of the battlefield and protected transportation routes from the rear areas. With the development of the operation, the lines of communication gradually lengthened. In order to protect these lines of communication it was necessary for several groups of fighter planes to patrol the areas for long periods of time. Often they were forced to engage the vastly superior enemy air forces raiding Japanese bases. By the end of July pilots of the 25th Air Regiment were flying from 80 to 120 hours a month. The best pilots as well as planes were gradually lost and could not be replaced. The fighter units did not engage the enemy other than when necessary in flying cover over the ground forces.

The Fifth Air Army had planned to use the 1st Air Brigade, in cooperation with other fighter units, to attack enemy air bases but due to the lack of general fighting power as well as the necessity to protect the long lines of communication, this plan was never carried out.

The Provisional Air Unit was assigned the mission of cooperating directly with the Eleventh Army. The air regiments of this unit were composed of Type 99 reconnaissance planes and Type 98 direct cooperation planes, both of which were inferior, out-dated planes. They did, however, cooperate closely with the front line divisions in locating the enemy and also acted as liaison between the different ground units during the intervals between enemy attacks. At first the Provisional Air Unit used Puchi and Pailochi airfields but, with the development of the operation, it advanced to Changsha and Hsiangtan. As soon as the Army occupied Hengyang airfield, the Air Unit, disregarding the strong enemy resistance still in the streets of Hengyang and the fact that the field was still under enemy fire, landed and closely cooperated with the Army in the battle for Hengyang.

At all times, this air unit advanced to airfields as close to the front lines as possible and closely cooperated with ground operations.

During the latter part of June the 2d Air Brigade Headquarters advanced to Canton when its 85th Air Regiment and other units cooperated with the ground operations of the Twenty-third Army. Cooperating with the main strength of the Fifth Air Army, the Brigade also raided enemy air bases at Kweilin, Liuchowhsien, Suichuan and Kanhsien at night in an endeavor to destroy the enemy air force on the ground.

The 16th and 90th Bomber Units, using Anyang and Tungshan as their main bases of operation and Wuchang and Hankou as their staging bases, when the necessity arose carried out night bombings on enemy air bases. It was not possible to carry out daylight raids with the outmoded Type 99 light bombers with which these units were equipped. However, the highly trained pilots compensated to some degree for the inferiority of their planes and their night dive - bombing attacks achieved excellent results. These attacks were made on moonlight nights against enemy air bases which were thought to be the most threatening. Those bases most often attacked were Suichuan, Kanhsien, Hengyang, Kweilin, Liuchowhsien, Chihkiang, Enshih, Liangshan and Laohokou. Although considerable damage was inflicted upon the enemy, continuous loss of planes and the tremendous build-up in enemy air strength, made it impossible to defeat them.

The 18th and 55th Reconnaissance Squadrons were responsible chiefly for locating enemy airfields against which night air attacks could be carried out and also for photographing and reconnoitering roads necessary for land operations.

Enemy Air Force Situation:

During the early part of May, it was estimated that the total number of airplanes at the front was approximately 520, composed of 340 United States Air Force planes, 100 United States-Chinese Air Force planes and 80 Chungking Air Army planes. Although the Fifth Air Army constantly attacked and inflicted heavy damage, the enemy received replacements in such large numbers that their strength continued to increase. It was estimated that they had increased to 600 planes by mid-June and 750 by mid-August.

The brunt of combat was borne by the United States Air Force with the United States-Chinese Air Force occasionally participating. It was believed that the Chungking Air Army was undergoing training as it was not encountered in the combat area.

An estimate of enemy air strength made during the Ichi-Go Operation was as shown on Chart No. 9. During the Peiping-Hankou Oper-

Chart No. 9

Estimated Disposition of the Enemy Air Strength in China
(May 1944 to December 1944)

Area Time	Southeast Area	Northwest Area	Szechwan Area	Yunnan Area
End of May	200	110	170	150
Beginning of June	150	120	160	160
Middle of July	120	70	180	140
Middle of August	130	120	340	160
Middle of December	116	136	194	290

Note: 1. Southeast area is the area southeast of Chihkiang; northwest area is the area north of Liangshan, Hancheng, and Laohokou.

2. The strength of the enemy air forces shown above was based upon estimates at that time and varies slightly from the figures given in the text.

ation the enemy temporarily reinforced its air strength in central and northwest China but with the advancement of the Hunan-Kwangsi Operation, it gradually shifted its strength to southeast China. With the occupation of Hengyang by the Eleventh Army, the enemy air force retreated to the Kweilin and Liuchowhsien districts. It strengthened the Chihkiang airfield and rapidly made it into a powerful advanced air base. From the point of view of air operations, Chihkiang was located on the flank of the Japanese operation and constituted a great obstacle to subsequent operations.

Enemy Attacks and Tactics:

The approximate number of attacks made and planes which participated in the Ichi-Go Operation are shown on Chart No. 10. Although the number of fighters and the time of attacks varied according to weather conditions and other circumstances, each succeeding month showed a steady increase in the number of attacks.

With the commencement of the Hunan-Kwangsi Operation, attacks rapidly increased in that area. It was characteristic of the entire Ichi-Go Operation that land troops depended on just one line of communications to penetrate a group of enemy air bases and, in consequence, lines of communications were always exposed to enemy attacks. The enemy air forces furiously attacked not only the front lines but also the rear transportation facilities in an effort to destroy lines of communication so that all movement, including ground troops, naval craft, automobiles, vehicles and trains were forced to move at night. It caused a marked decrease in transportation capacity and, as the battle situation developed, transportation of supplies to the front became more and more difficult.

During the day the enemy used mostly P-51's and P-40's to attack front line units and also to destroy rear transportation facilities. Daylight attacks were seldom launched against the Wu-Han sector but occasionally the advance base at Pailochi was subjected to surprise raids. At night B-24's attacked Pailochi and Wu-Han in an effort to destroy the depots and warehouses in this area.

From the Fall of Hengyang to the End of Ichi-Go Operation
General Situation of Ground Operations:

The Eleventh Army, following the capture of Hengyang, consolidated its forces to the rear and prepared to launch an attack against Kweilin. Meanwhile, the Twenty-third Army advanced from the area along the Hsi Chiang and prepared for operations in the Liuchowhsien area.

In early November, these two armies succeeded in achieving the first objective of the Ichi-Go Operation by capturing Kweilin and Liuchowhsien.

In January 1945, the Twentieth and Twenty-third Armies began operations to control the area along the southern Canton-Hankou railway and occupy enemy air bases in the Suichuan-Kanhsien area. By 26 January, the

Chart No. 10

Enemy Attacks May 1944 – October 1944

Districts / Period	North China	Central China	South China	Formosa	French Indo-China	Thailand	East China Sea	Total
Early May	10 (40)	19 (162)	5 (6)	2 (5)				36 (213)
Mid-May	10 (90)	17 (140)	2 (5)		9 (50)	1 (16)	every day 5-6 planes	39 (300)
Late May	20 (85)	26 (235)	8 (10)		4 (11)			58 (341)
Early Jun	20 (100)	60 (400)	17 (38)					97 (538)
Mid-Jun	51 (205)	80 (524)	12 (17)	10 (11)	12 (24)			155 (770)
Late Jun	12 (55)	91 (535)	7 (11)	1 (1)	5 (8)			125 (620)
Early Jul	9 (13)	181 (1,080)	34 (150)		A few			225 (1,270)
Mid-Jul	13 (106)	120 (775)	22 (129)					155 (1,000)
Early Aug	10 (60)	136 (972)	16 (40)	1 (1)				163 (1,073)
Mid-Aug	18 (64)	171 (1,007)	21 (40)	5 (85)	4 (7)			219 (1,203)

Chart No. 10

Enemy Attacks (cont'd)

Districts / Period	North China	Central China	South China	Formosa	French Indo-China	Thailand	East China Sea	Total
Late Aug	16 (65)	162 (832)	24 (85)	7 (15)	4 (12)			213 (1,009)
Mid-Sep	7 (18)	108 (671)	24 (124)	2 (4)				141 (813)
Late Sep	10 (61)	44 (287)	22 (157)	5 (96)	14 (43)			95 (644)
Early Oct	38	122	175		7			342
Mid-Oct	38		692	206	21			989

Remarks:
1. The figures quoted for China are those confirmed by the China Expeditionary Army. Those outside China are confined to those reported to the Army.
2. B-29's raids on Japan and Manchuria were omitted from this list.
3. Number of planes shown in parenthesis.

entire Canton-Hankou railway line had been captured and, by 8 February, all airfields in the Suichuan-Kanhsien area were occupied. Thus the Ichi-Go Operation was brought to a successful conclusion.

Fifth Air Army Situation:

The disposition and missions of the various elements of the Fifth Air Army from the fall of Hengyang to the occupation of Liuchowhsien were as shown on Chart No. 11.

The decline in strength of the Air Army, especially fighter strength, during the operations prior to the capture of Hengyang was considerable. This, coupled with the fact that B-29's based around Chengtu were bombing Japan and Manchuria, made it imperative that air strength be built up in China and efforts to destroy the enemy air force intensified. Imperial General Headquarters, therefore, assigned three air regiments (22d and 29th Regiments (fighters) and the 60th Regiment (heavy bombers))[7] to the China Expeditionary Army for a period of one month, from the latter part of August.

The 22d Air Regiment, equipped with Type 4 fighters, manned by veteran pilots, the best the Army Air Force had, proved of great help to the Air Army. Meanwhile, during the period from the capture of Hengyang to the opening of operations against Kweilin, other air

---

7. The 22d and 60th Regiments were transferred from the First Air Army in Japan while the 29th Regiment was transferred from the 8th Air Division in Formosa.

units exerted every effort to restore their fighting power. With the withdrawal of the reinforcements, however, Japanese air power in China proved vastly inferior to that of the enemy.

The number of serviceable planes of the various air units around mid-November was:

    9th Air Regiment: 5 Type 2 fighters
    25th Air Regiment: 9 Type 1 fighters
                               3 Type 4 fighters
    48th Air Regiment: 2 Type 1 fighters
    85th Air Regiment: 17 Type 2 fighters
                               10 Type 4 fighters
    16th Air Regiment: 20 light bombers
                               2 biplane fighters
    90th Air Regiment: 18 light bombers
    44th Air Regiment: 17 direct cooperation planes
                               15 reconnaissance planes
    54th Independent Air Squadron: 7 direct cooperation planes
                                              3 reconnaissance planes
    6th Regiment: 16 assault planes
    82d Air Regiment: 8 Headquarters reconnaissance planes
              Total: 152 airplanes

Chart No. 11

Disposition and Mission of the Fifth Air Army
(From the time of the attack on Hengyang to the Occupation of Liuchowhsien)

Tactical Organization		Type of Plane	Airfield	Mission
1st Air Brigade	1st Air Brigade Headquarters		Pailochi	1. Air defense of the Hunan-Kwangsi Operation Area. 2. Protection of Bomber Units which were to Directly Cooperate with ground force.
	25th Air Regiment	Type 1 Fighter		
	48th Air Regiment	Type 1 Fighter	(Wu-Han - Hankou Area)	
	22d Air Regiment	Type 4 Fighter		
	29th Air Regiment	Type 2 Fighter		
2d Air Brigade	2d Air Brigade Headquarters		Canton	1. Direct Cooperation with the Twenty-third Army. 2. Air defense of strategic points in Canton area. 3. Decisive air battles.
	85th Air Regiment	Type 2 Fighter & Type 4 Fighter		
	Part of the 6th Air Regiment	Type 99 Attack Planes		
	Part of the 44th Air Regiment	Direct Co-operation Planes		
	Part of the 90th Air Regiment	Light Bomber		
	18th Independent Air Squadron	Headquarters' Reconnaissance Planes		

170

Disposition and Mission of the Fifth Air Army (cont'd)

Chart No. 11

Tactical Organization		Type of Plane	Airfield	Mission
The 8th Air Brigade	8th Air Brigade Headquarters		Hankou	1. Decisive air battles. 2. Protection of vessels on the Yangtze River from Hsiaochihkou to the vicinity of Hankou in the upper areas of the river. 3. Air Defense of Wu-Han area.
	9th Air Regiment	Type 2 Fighter	Hsinhsiang	
	16th Air Regiment	Twin-engined light bomber	Wuchang	
	90th Air Regiment (minus one part)	Twin-engined light bomber	Hankou	
	60th Air Regiment	Heavy bomber	Nanching (Hankou)	
Directly controlled units	The 44th Air Regiment (minus one part but including the 54th Independent Air Squadron)	Reconnaissance and direct co-operation planes	Hengyang	Direct cooperation with Eleventh Army.
	6th Air Regiment (minus one part)	Type 99 Attack planes	Hengyang	
	18th Independent Air Squadron (minus one part)	Headquarters Reconnaissance planes	Hankou	Location of Enemy Fields.
	55th Independent Air Squadron	Headquarters Reconnaissance planes	Hankou	

Remarks:
1. The 22d, 29th and 60th Air Regiments were scheduled to be placed under the command of the Fifth Air Army for about one month beginning the latter part of August.
2. At the end of the period, the 9th Air Regiment was placed under the command of the 2d Air Brigade and the 85th Air Regiment under the command of the 1st Air Brigade.
3. Parentheses indicate staging airfields.
4. The Air Training Units in charge of the air defense at strategic points is omitted.

The ratio of Japanese air strength as compared to the enemy's at the beginning of the operation was 1 to 2 but by the time the operation against Kweilin was launched it had dropped to 1 to 5.3. The skill of the pilots of the 25th Air Regiment who fought on the most important fronts during the Ichi-Go Operation was estimated to be:

	A	B	C	Total
31 May	31	7	6	44
31 August	19	6	0	25

A, B and C denote the degree of skill based on experience and flying hours. The number of pilots includes officers, warrant officers and non-commissioned officers. The six "Type C" pilots shown as of 31 May were later transferred to the B class after training. Similar conditions existed in other air units (Chart No. 12). Further, as veteran pilots were continually lost they were replaced by inexperienced men who had just completed basic training, so that the skill of the pilots dropped rapidly in quality. The supply of planes and parts from Japan proved inadequate, making it necessary to put back into service even obsolete planes, which previously had been used as trainers at the rear. Loss of planes due to mechanical failure became increasingly frequent and it was extremely difficult for the air units to use their strength effectively.

Tactical Command:

In order to restore its fighting power after the capture of Hengyang, the main force of the Fifth Air Army was concentrated in the Wu-Han sector. Repairs to the airfield, as well as the construction of fuel storage facilities and ammunitions dumps were stepped up. However, the unusually long rainy season during September and October turned the area into a sea of mud and made transportation extremely difficult. Nevertheless, by early November large stocks of fuel and ammunition were assembled in the vicinity of Hengyang in readiness for the next operation. Radar was not yet effective in the field. It was necessary, therefore, to establish observation posts. As these posts were limited to a radius of 70 km of Hengyang, they proved inadequate and there was constant danger of enemy surprise raids. As Chihkiang, an advance enemy base, was only 300 km from Hengyang, it was recognized that there was every possibility of Hengyang airfields being subjected to enemy air attacks after the operation began.

With the opening of the attack against Kweilin and Liuchowhsien at the beginning of November, the Fifth Air Army, in order to support the Eleventh and Twenty-third Armies, deployed the 1st Air Brigade at Pailochi and Hengyang, the 2d Air Brigade at Canton, Wuchow and Tanchuhsu, the 8th Air Brigade at Wuchang, and the 6th and 44th Air Regiments together with the 54th Independent Air Squadron at Hengyang and Lingling.

Chart No. 12

Number and Skill of Pilots of the Fifth Air Army

Reported end August 1944

Classification	Officers						Non-Commissioned Officers and Enlisted Men					
	Authorized Personnel	Assigned					Authorized Personnel	Assigned				
Unit number		A	B	C	Total			A	B	C	Total	
9th Air Regiment	13	5	1		6		30	6	4	20	30	
22d Air Regiment*	13	9			9		30	12	17		29	
25th Air Regiment	13	9			9		30	10	6		16	
29th Air Regiment*	13	5			5		30	5	10		15	
48th Air Regiment	13	3			3		30	1	16	6	23	
85th Air Regiment	13	5			5		30	5	20	9	34	
16th Air Regiment	9	10			10		27	14	10		24	
90th Air Regiment	9	7	2		9		27	8	9	1	18	
6th Air Regiment	13	8			8		24	6	11		17	
44th Air Regiment	6	6	2	7	15		20	13	3		16	
60th Air Regiment*	9	12			12		27	11	18	4	33	
18th Independent Air Squadron	3	4			4		5	11			11	
54th Independent Air Squadron	0	1	2		3		9	5	2	1	8	

Number and Skill of Pilots of the Fifth Air Army (cont'd)

Chart No. 12

Classification / Unit number	Officers						Non-Commissioned Officers and Enlisted Men				
	Authorized Personnel	Assigned					Authorized Personnel	Assigned			
		A	B	C	Total			A	B	C	Total
55th Independent Air Squadron	3	2		3	5		5	6		2	8
Total	130				103		324				282

Remarks: 1. Air Training Units not included.

2. Hospitalized personnel are not included in this chart.

3. A, B and C are unofficial classifications of ability based on experience and number of flying hours.

4. * Temporarily attached unit.

After the main force of the 1st Air Brigade had advanced to Hengyang, the entire enemy air force attacked Hengyang airfield and commenced an extensive air battle. The 1st Air Brigade was at a great disadvantage as the Hengyang airfield, due to its inferior communications system and lack of airplane repairing facilities, did not function very satisfactorily, while, on the other hand, the enemy's air base at Chihkiang was very well equipped. The Brigade commander, therefore, ordered the Brigade to return to Pailochi and continue its mission from there.

Even after the capture of Kweilin and Liuchowhsien, enemy planes continued to use Suichuan and Kanhsien as advance bases from which to attack the Japanese rear areas. They successfully attacked ships on the Yangtze River and made surprise attacks on the Canton district. In conjunction with the operation to open the southern portion of the Canton-Hankou railway, therefore, it was decided to destroy the bases at Suichuan and Kanhsien.

Part of the 2d Air Brigade, the 6th Air Regiment, the 44th Air Regiment and the 54th Independent Air Squadron, using airfields in the Canton area as well as bases at Hengyang and Leiyang, took part in this operation (3 Jan - 8 Feb 1945) while the remaining force of the Fifth Air Army reorganized its fighting strength in the rear areas.

The Fifth Air Army commander then decided to repair and complete the airfields at Hengyang, Lingling, Kweilin, Liuchowhsien, Kanhsien, Hsincheng and Nanhsiung and to establish air base groups in preparation for attacks on the southwest hinterlands. Staging bases were to be established in the rear areas to prevent attempted enemy landings in the south China area and an air base was to be established for liaison between central and south China. A base for liaison between central and south China was considered very necessary as the corridor occupied by the ground forces was extremely narrow and the intelligence relay network between bases was very poor. Further, due to inadequate transportation facilities from the rear areas, the accumulation of fuel and ammunition progressed very slowly. The bases, therefore, were no more than connecting airfields until the end of the operation.

Outline of Operations by Fifth Air Army Units:

The 1st Air Brigade, which was stationed at Pailochi airfield, and was responsible for the protection of transportation facilities in the rear area, had advanced to Hengyang during the attack on Kweilin and had engaged in bitter fighting with the enemy air force. Later, it returned to Pailochi airfield and cooperated with the ground forces. After the capture of Kweilin and Liuchowhsien by the ground forces, the Brigade endeavored to strengthen its fighting power by intensive training in the Wu-Han district.

The 2d Air Brigade closely cooperated with the Twenty-third

Army's operation and, simultaneous with the Army's advance advanced its bases to Wuchow and Tanchuhsu. The Brigade then moved forward to Liuchowhsien airfield and was particularly active in giving direct support to the front line units during the pursuit operation in the area west of Liuchowhsien. At the same time, part of its light bomber unit carried out repeated night attacks against enemy air bases in the area.

The 8th Air Brigade continued its night attacks on Kweilin, Liuchowhsien, Chihkiang, Laohokou, Liangshan, Suichuan and Kanhsien. After the loss of Hengyang, Kweilin and Liuchowhsien airfields, the enemy moved its advanced air base to Chihkiang and the Brigade, at opportune times, made repeated attacks against this base.

The main forces of the 6th and 44th Air Regiments and the 54th Independent Air Squadron were stationed at the Hengyang air base. When required, part of these units advanced to Lingling and closely cooperated with the Eleventh Army. In spite of the enemy's air superiority, by skilfully camouflaging their planes and taking advantage of the intervals between the enemy attacks, weather conditions and dawn and twilight, they rendered great service in direct cooperation with the Army's operation.

Enemy Air Force Situation:

The enemy air force was not active during September and October. It was presumed that this was due to the fact that they were preparing for the next operation as well as to the continued bad weather. As the Japanese ground forces closed in on Kweilin and Liuchowhsien, the enemy destroyed their airfields and retreated into the interior. Prior to this, the enemy had made strenuous efforts to consolidate its forces at Chihkiang and the strategical and tactical value of this field rapidly increased as, with its withdrawal from Kweilin and Liuchowhsien, it moved its advanced base to Chihkiang.

At the beginning of November, as the Eleventh and Twenty-third Armies closed in on Kweilin and Liuchowhsien, the enemy air force from Chihkiang made fierce attacks against the Japanese rear area transport facilities and front line units and kept the lines of communication under constant pressure. Using the airfields in the Suichuan and Kanhsien districts as staging bases, it made surprise attacks on vessels in the Yangtze River and the rear air bases at Canton and Nanching. With the progress of the operation to destroy the air bases in the Suichuan and Kanhsien districts, the enemy, after destroying these air bases, retreated. Thus, enemy air bases in southeast China were completely destroyed. The enemy, however, continued night bombing attacks on Wuchang and Hankou and aerial mine-laying in the Yangtze River. They also began to make daylight attacks, mainly by fighter planes, on strategic points along the Tienching-Pukou railway.

Furthermore, the enemy air force made furious daylight attacks on the Hunan-Kwangsi area, the focal point of the operation. It was reinforced and began attacks on such important air bases in the rear areas as Hankou, Nanching, Shanghai, Licheng and Peiping as well as continuing its attacks against the district along the Tienching-Pukou railway and the area to the west of the line.

Estimates on B-29's:

Great publicity had been given to the stepped-up production of the United States' B-29 long-distance bombers and it was estimated that the time was not far distant when the enemy, using these planes, would commence large-scale bombing attacks on Japan and Manchuria from bases in China. From intelligence reports it appeared that Chengtu was being prepared as a base for the B-29's. It was estimated, however, that raids on Japan from bases in China would be confined to western Japan and that, even if this area were badly damaged, it would in no way curtail Japan's ability to wage war.

At the time of the opening of Ichi-Go Operation, because of the limited range of the Type 100 Headquarters reconnaissance planes, it was difficult to reconnoiter Chengtu and its surrounding area. It was difficult, therefore, to obtain exact information in regard to the B-29's but it was believed that, at the beginning of May, about ten of these planes were stationed at Chengtu and its vicinity and that they were constantly shuttling between India and China where a considerable number of B-29's were stationed. Judging from information received in regard to the training of crews for these planes, the rapid accumulation of fuel in the area and the progress of equipping the air base at Chengtu, it was estimated that air raids by B-29's on Japan and Manchuria would be possible by the end of May. Furthermore, it appeared as though the enemy was stepping-up preparations for this operation.

On the night of 15 June 1944, B-29's, taking off from Chengtu, raided Moji and Yawata. This was the first air raid by B-29's on Japan. Thereafter, until they were transferred to Saipan in June 1945, B-29's continued to raid west Japan, Manchuria and Formosa from the Chengtu base.

Although the exact number of B-29's in China could not be confirmed at any given time, it was estimated that in mid-August 1944 the number was approximately 150 and in early October approximately 200.

Intelligence Network to Cope with B-29's:

Prior to the appearance of the B-29's, air intelligence had functioned as part of the air defense system of the Japanese Army but this system proved inadequate to cope with B-29 raids on Japan, Manchuria and Formosa from bases in China.

In order to improve and strengthen the air intelligence system so that it might not only alert the areas concerned but also trace the course of the B-29's moment by moment and aid the interceptors in the air over China, observation posts along the Peiping-Hankou and Tienching-Pukou railways were increased and an additional amount of radar equipment was installed at **strategic** points in north and central China.

It was found, however, that after the radar equipment was installed it took some time to adjust before it was fully effective and further, due to the limited number of signal units and the vast area involved, the number of observation posts established were inadequate. In addition, the area between the two railway lines was held by the enemy so that no air intelligence could be obtained from there. Consequently, plotting the course of the B-29 flights and the direction of the interceptor planes was often delayed and inaccurate. Later, a system was devised whereby air intelligence reports concerning B-29's were transmitted directly to Japan which, in turn, issued warnings to units within Japan, Manchuria and Formosa. In time, this method became efficient and generally served its purpose.

Interception

With the advent of the B-29's, some of the fighter units assigned to the Ichi-Go Operation as well as some interceptor fighter units organized from part of the air training units with instructors as pilots, were diverted to intercept these enemy planes en route.

When air intelligence reported the approach of B-29's, the disposition of the interceptor units was determined by the general situation at the time, weather conditions and the time of day, usually in the vicinity of the Peiping-Hankou or the Tienching-Pukou railway. However, as mentioned previously, the gathering and relaying of air intelligence was unsatisfactory and the interceptor fighters often patrolled the air over the estimated course of the enemy bombers in the hope of intercepting enemy planes. Repeated attacks by the fighters were generally difficult due to the inefficiency of the planes. Interception, therefore, was not very effective. Headquarters reconnaissance planes and light bombers were used to spot the planes, but since these planes were not equipped with radar the search had to be made with the naked eye. This method was far from satisfactory. In consequence, interceptor fighters often took to the air on false reports and failed to contact the enemy planes. Under these circumstances, the fighter units which had been severely damaged during the Ichi-Go Operation, deteriorated still further.

Air Raids Over Bases in Chengtu

With the appearance of the B-29's, the need for bombing enemy air bases in the vicinity of Chengtu became vital and the Fifth Air Army made the following preparations:

a. Auxiliary tanks were installed in the twin-engine Type 99 light bombers for long-range attacks. As both the 16th and 90th Air Regiments were equipped with these outmoded twin-engine Type 99 light bombers and there was no hope of their being replaced by newer type planes, it was decided to use these planes for night bombing with every effort being made to increase their cruising range.

The planes were equipped with auxiliary tanks inside the fuselage with all arms unnecessary for night bombing being dismantled. At the same time, the number of persons aboard each plane was reduced to three. This made it possible to use these planes for night bombing raids within a radius of 1,100 km.

b. Both regiments practiced exclusively for night bombing and received training in radio guide beam and long-range navigation.

When the B-29's began bombing raids over Japan and Manchuria, the Fifth Air Army awaited an opportunity to carry out counterattacks. On the night of 8 September, eight heavy bombers and ten twin-engine light bombers of the 8th Air Brigade bombed the airfields around Chengtu for the first time. They burnt seven B-29's and destroyed eleven others on the ground. In addition, they started fires in four different places. Two of the heavy bombers were reported missing in action.

These attacks were repeated and continued whenever the concentration of planes justified and weather and moonlight permitted as long as Chengtu was used as a B-29 base.

CHAPTER 9

Preparations for Operations Along the China Coast

January - August 1945

Japanese Air Force Situation

During the Hunan-Kwangsi and Suichuan-Kanhsien operations enemy air bases in southwestern China had been wiped out. However, strong enemy air forces based in Chihkiang in central China and Laohokou in northern China continued to harass the Japanese forces and to strike at the railroads and motor highways in north and central China and the occupied areas along Yangtze River and Hsiang Chiang in central China. At the same time, the enemy was receiving large air shipments of munitions and personnel and there were very definite indications that they planned to launch a major counteroffensive.

Due to heavy plane losses in the Philippines and Okinawan campaigns, Imperial General Headquarters foresaw the impossibility of replenishing anticipated plane losses in China during 1945. In an effort to check the enemy air force, therefore, Imperial General Headquarters ordered the China Expeditionary Army to destroy the enemy airfields in the Laohokou and Chihkiang sectors. Although Air Force participation in these operations was limited to reconnaissance and direct cooperation, since the objective of both operations was the destruction of enemy air bases, their successful conclusion was of great importance to the Air Force.

Two reconnaissance squadrons of the 44th Air Regiment, using air bases at Chenghsien and Hsuchang, supported the Twelfth Army during the Laohokou Operation, while direct cooperation planes of the 54th Independent Squadron, from Hengyang and Shaoyang, supported the Twentieth Army's Chihkiang Operation.

Enemy Air Force Situation

Prior to 1945, the attacking enemy aircraft had used bases in the interior of China but after the turn of the year enemy planes from bases in the Philippines and later from Okinawa as well as planes from aircraft carriers participated in the attacks on the Japanese forces in China.

It was estimated that the number of enemy front line planes based in China in July 1945 was somewhere in the vicinity of 1,100 planes.[1] (See Chart No. 13) It was thought that the main force of about 600 planes was based in the northwestern area and around Chungking and Chengtu and operated over north and central China, while about 200 planes were based in the southwestern area and a further 300 in the vicinity of Kunming. In addition, planes were based around Suichuan and Kanhsien in the southeastern area, which operated over Nanching and along the Yangtze River.

---

1. In Chapter 5, Monograph No. 72, Army Operations in China, Jan 1944 - Aug 1945, the number of enemy planes in China in April 1945 is given as between 1500 and 2000. This was an Army estimate of the total number of enemy planes in China, whereas the Air Force estimate of 1,100 planes in July 1945 does not include planes held in reserve to be used later as reinforcements or replenishments, or planes being serviced or repaired.

Direction of Operations and Tactics

It was believed that the enemy's main objective in air operations at this time was to cut the Japanese land and sea communications in order to isolate the China Expeditionary Army. B-24's and other enemy planes conducted round-the-clock patrols over the sea and attacked even the smallest Japanese vessel in order to complete the blockade. As a result, after March sea communications over the East China Sea were at an almost complete standstill.

On land, attacks were centered in north and central China where the P-51 and P-47 fighters concentrated on attacking rolling stock and other vital transportation targets. Occasionally, these planes attacked lines of communication in the rear areas. They seriously damaged the railway system and made it almost impossible to operate it during the day.

The enemy air force continued to reinforce its strength in advanced air bases in the vicinity of Changan, Laohokou, Ankang, Liangshan and Enshih. This, together with the increased efficiency of the P-51's (their range of operations covered all of north and central China and enabled them to operate from dawn to dusk) meant that the air over China was dominated by the enemy air force during the day, not only completely disrupting land transportation but also preventing air movements and air training.

While enemy air strength increased, Japanese air strength de-

Chart No. 13

Estimated Disposition of Enemy Front-line Planes in China

20 July 1945

District	Locality	P-38	P-40 P-51	P-47	P-61	B-25	B-24	Total
Northwestern Area	Changan	2	22 (15)	8	1			33 (15)
	Nancheng	6	33	27	1	22	11	100
	Ankang		21	16	1	3		41
	Liangshan	2	47		2	17		69
	Enshih		12 (29)					12 (29)
								255 (44)
Southwestern Area	Chihkiang	3	43			6		52
	Laohwangping	4	48					52
	Kweiyang		(30)					(30)
	Tuhshan		19		2			19
	Tsingchen		17					19
	Paise	2	8					10
	Nanning	1	7			2		10
	Liuchowhsien		24					24
								186 (30)

188

Chart No. 13

Estimated Disposition of Enemy Front-line Planes in China (cont'd)

District	Locality	P-38	P-40 P-51	P-47	P-61	B-25	B-24	Total	
Chungking–Chengtu Area	Laifengyi	2	3					5	252 (50)
	Chengtu	1	45 (15)	98 (?)	5	29 (13)		178 (28)	
	Paishihiyi	6	32 (22)		21 (?)	2	5	66 (22)	
	Suining		1		2			3	
Yunnan Area	Chaotung		1					1	255 (19)
	Kunming	2	40 (1)		3	10	8	63 (1)	
	Luliang	10	10			13 (18)		33 (18)	
	Chengkung	10	15			3	13	41	
	Chanyi	2	1			2		5	
	Yangchieh					47		47	
	Poshan		14					14	
	Mengtzu	23	13					36	
	Yunnanyi		15					15	
Total		76	492 (112)	149	38	156 (31)	37	948 (143)	Grand Total 1,091

Remarks: 1. Figures in parentheses indicate Chinese air force.
2. ? Indicates figures doubtful.

creased without hope of replenishment. In consequence, enemy movements became bolder and more active.

Attacks from the Sea

With the establishment of enemy air bases in the Philippines and Okinawa, enemy planes patrolled the coast of east China and attacked Shanghai and Canton areas.

Beginning in June, the enemy air force based on Okinawa, as well as task forces, attacked Shanghai and the Chushan Archipelago, inflicting heavy damage on the base installations and harbors. As it was impossible for the Japanese Air Force to repulse these attacks, in order to minimize losses, whenever the enemy attacked, planes based in the triangular zone were transferred to the interior. It was believed that these large-scale attacks were conducted solely by planes based outside China.

Fifth Air Army's Preparations Against Attacks from the Sea

In early 1945, with the rapid deterioration of the war situation in the Pacific, attacks on Japan and the China coast from the sea seemed inevitable. Imperial General Headquarters, therefore, ordered the China Expeditionary Army to strengthen strategic areas in China in preparation for any attempted invasion by the United States forces.

The main force of the Fifth Air Army, which had been reorganizing its fighting power in the vicinity of Wuchang and Hankou, by the end of January was concentrated in the triangular zone (the area between Shanghai, Hangchou and Nanching) where it endeavored to regain its fighting strength by intensive training, particularly in fighting over water.

Operational preparations in southeast China were under the supervision of the 2d Air Brigade based in the Canton area. The Brigade was responsible for the repairing and strengthening of established airfields, especially runways; the establishing of bomb-proof shelters and strengthening of repair facilities; the dispersal of fuel storage facilities and ammunition dumps and the strengthening of communication and information systems.

Owing to the difficulty in securing the required materials, the repairing and strengthening of the fields did not proceed as planned. The use of the airfields was further restricted by the rainy season, but other operational preparations were completed temporarily by March.

Organization of the 13th Air Division

In order to assist in the complex duties of the Fifth Air Army in preparing to meet attacks from the sea, as well as from United States and Chinese Air Forces based in China, and, at the same time, give direct cooperation to land operations, the 13th Air Division was organized and, on 6 March, placed in the order of battle of the

Fifth Air Army. The Division's headquarters was located at Hankou and its chief missions were operational preparations against enemy attacks from the east and south sea fronts and cooperation in operations against the interior.

With the rapid advance of the United States forces and their landing on Okinawa, both Japan and Korea were exposed to the danger of American landings. On 15 May, therefore, the main force of the Fifth Air Army was removed from the order of battle of the China Expeditionary Army and placed in that of the General Air Army. The Fifth Air Army was then transferred to Korea with headquarters in Seoul. Air units in China north of the Lunghai Railway however remained under the command of the commander of the Fifth Air Army.[2]

At the same time the headquarters of the 13th Air Division was moved to Nanching and those air units in China below the Lunghai Railway were placed under the command of the commander of the Division. They were:

13th Air Division	Nanching
3d Air Brigade HQ	Nanching

---

2. It is difficult to state what units were in north China or Korea at any given time as units (or elements of units) shuttled between bases according to the exigency of the situation. Bases in north China were used as rear bases for units in Korea and also as training areas for pilots. While there were many large fields in north China and south Manchuria, there were very few usable airfields in Korea.

9th Air Regiment	Type 2 single-seater fighters / Type 4 fighters	15 planes, Nanching
48th Air Regiment	Type 1 fighters	20 planes, Taihsien
90th Air Regiment	Type 99 twin-engine light bombers	25 planes, Licheng
One squadron of the 44th Air Regiment	Type 99 reconnaisance planes	8 planes, Wuchin
54th Independent Squadron	Type 98 direct cooperation planes	10 planes, Hangchou
Part of the 81st Air Regiment	Type 100 reconnaissance planes	4 planes, Nanching

N.B. The number of planes is approximate as they were given from memory.

Preparations for Air Operations in Central and North China

About February preparations for air operations in central and north China gradually got under way. The Fifth Air Army continued to supervise preparations for operations in north China while those in central China became the responsibility of the 13th Air Division. Judging that the American forces would first attack Shanghai and its vicinity, emphasis was placed on operations in cooperation with the local ground and naval units in the triangular zone.

Following the diversion of the main force of the Fifth Air Army to Korea, the strength of the air force in China was considerably decreased. In June or July, therefore, approximately 200 special attack planes (suicide planes) from Manchuria and Korea were attached to the 13th Air Division. The pilots of these planes, together with those of the other air units, then underwent training for special attacks and combat over the sea.

In order that operations might be continued in the triangular zone, even under severe enemy raids, the repair and enlargement of the principal airfields, the construction of bombproof installations and the establishment of concealed airfields was undertaken.

Main Points of the Operational Plan to Protect the China Coast

Method:

    The primary mission of the 13th Air Division is to destroy enemy transport convoys at sea. Should the convoys succeed in landing, the Division will cooperate directly with the ground force operations.

    As the main enemy landing is expected to be made in the downstream area of the Yangtze River, emphasis on operational preparations will be placed on the triangular zone.

Direction:

    The 13th Air Division, maintaining close liaison with the Army and Navy, will collect and evaluate information in regard to enemy movements that will assist in the early detection of enemy landings.

    The Air Division will patrol important areas during essential periods (particular attention will be given to the direction of Okinawa) in order to locate enemy task forces and transport convoys.

    Upon evidence of an imminent enemy raid

the main units of the air force in the triangular zone will withdraw to the interior in order to prevent plane losses.

In the event the enemy lands in the area north of Ningpo, the entire force of the 13th Air Division will be employed to attack the enemy. Should the enemy land in the area south of Yungchia, only part of the Air Division will be used in the attack. Should the enemy invade the south China area, reconnaissance units of the Air Division will cooperate directly with the Twenty-third Army's operation.

Every opportunity will be taken to attack enemy transport convoys at sea and, should the opportunity arise, special attack planes will be used to attack enemy aircraft carriers.

Details of the battle plan, should the enemy attack in the vicinity of Shanghai, are described below.

Disposition of Forces:

In accordance with the enemy's direction of attack, the commander of the 3d Air Brigade may unite and command all air forces, or the main force of the Division may remain under the direct command of the Division commander with part of the force under the command of the 3d Air Brigade commander.

Composition and extent of training of Special Attack Units, in mid-August, is shown on Chart No. 14.

Battle Plan of 13th Air Division in the Event of an Enemy Attack in the Vicinity of Shanghai

The Plan:

In the event of an enemy attack against Chushan Archipelago or in the vicinity of Shanghai, the 13th Air Division will establish its main bases of departure at Suchou and Hangchou

Chart No. 14

Special Attack Units

August 1945

Assigned Unit	Special Attack Unit	Types of Planes	Number of Planes	Extent of Training	Training Ground of Main Force
	Sakigake (TN Spearhead) 1st Air Unit	Type 2 single-seat fighter	6	Capable of taking action in moonlight	Nanching
	Sakigake 2d Air Unit	Type 4 fighter	6	Capable of taking action in moonlight	
	Sakigake 11th Air Unit	Type 1 fighter	12	Capable of taking action at dawn and dusk	
9th Air Regiment	Sakigake 12th Air Unit	Type 1 fighter	12	Capable of taking action at dawn and dusk	
	Special 133d Air Unit	Type 1 fighter	6	Capable of taking action at dawn and dusk	
	Special 443d Air Unit	Type 95 Intermediate trainer	15	Capable of taking action at dawn and dusk	
	Sakigake 3d Air Unit	Type 1 fighter	6	Capable of taking action in moonlight	
48th Air Regiment	Sakigake 4th Air Unit	Type 1 fighter	6	Capable of taking action in moonlight	Taihsien
	Sakigake 13th Air Unit	Type 1 fighter	6	Capable of taking action at dawn and dusk	
	Special 223d Air Unit	Type 98 direct cooperation plane	6	Capable of taking action at dawn and dusk	

Chart No. 14

Special Attack Units (cont'd)   August 1945

Assigned Unit	Special Attack Unit	Types of Planes	Number of Planes	Extent of Training	Training Ground of Main Force
48th Air Regiment (cont'd)	Special 224th Air Unit	Type 97 fighter	6	Capable of taking action at dawn and dusk	
	Special 251st Air Unit	Type 1 fighter	6	Capable of taking action at dawn and dusk	
	Special 252d Air Unit	Type 2 single-seat fighter	6	Capable of taking action in moonlight	
	Sakigake 5th Air Unit	Type 99 twin-engined light bomber	6	Capable of taking action in dark night	
	Sakigake 6th Air Unit	Type 99 twin-engined light bomber	6	Capable of taking action in dark night	Licheng
	Sakigake 14th Air Unit	Type 99 twin-engined light bomber	6	Capable of taking action in moonlight	
90th Air Regiment	Sakigake 15th Air Unit	Type 99 twin-engined light bomber	6	Capable of taking action in moonlight	
	Sakigake 16th Air Unit	Type 99 twin-engined light bomber	6	Capable of taking action in moonlight	
	Special 306th Air Unit	Type 1 twin-engined Advance Trainer	6	Capable of taking action in moonlight	
	Special 441st Air Unit	Type 95 Intermediate Trainer	15	Capable of taking action at dawn and dusk	

Chart No. 14

Special Attack Units (cont'd)   August 1945

Assigned Unit	Special Attack Unit	Types of Planes	Number of Planes	Extent of Training	Training Ground of Main Force
	Sakigake 7th Air Unit	Type 99 Reconnaissance plane	4	Capable of taking action in moonlight	
2d Squadron of the 44th Air Regiment	Sakigake 17th Air Unit	Type 98 direct co-operation plane	6	Capable of taking action at dawn and dusk	
	Special 345th Air Unit	Type 95 Intermediate trainer	14	Capable of taking action at dawn and dusk	Wuchin
	Special 436th Air Unit	Type 95 Intermediate trainer	15	Capable of taking action at dawn and dusk	
	Special 437th Air Unit	Type 95 Intermediate trainer	15	Capable of taking action at dawn and dusk	
	Sakigake 8th Air Unit	Type 98 direct co-operation plane	4	Capable of taking action in moonlight	
54th Independent Air Squadron	Special 126th Air Unit	Type 98 direct co-operation plane	6	Capable of taking action in daylight	
	Special 127th Air Unit	Type 98 direct co-operation plane	6	Capable of taking action in daylight	Hangchou
	Special 437th Air Unit	Type 95 Intermediate trainer	15	Capable of taking action at dawn and dusk	
	Special 439th Air Unit	Type 95 Intermediate trainer	15	Capable of taking action at dawn and dusk	
	Special 440th Air Unit	Type 95 Intermediate trainer	15	Capable of taking action at dawn and dusk	

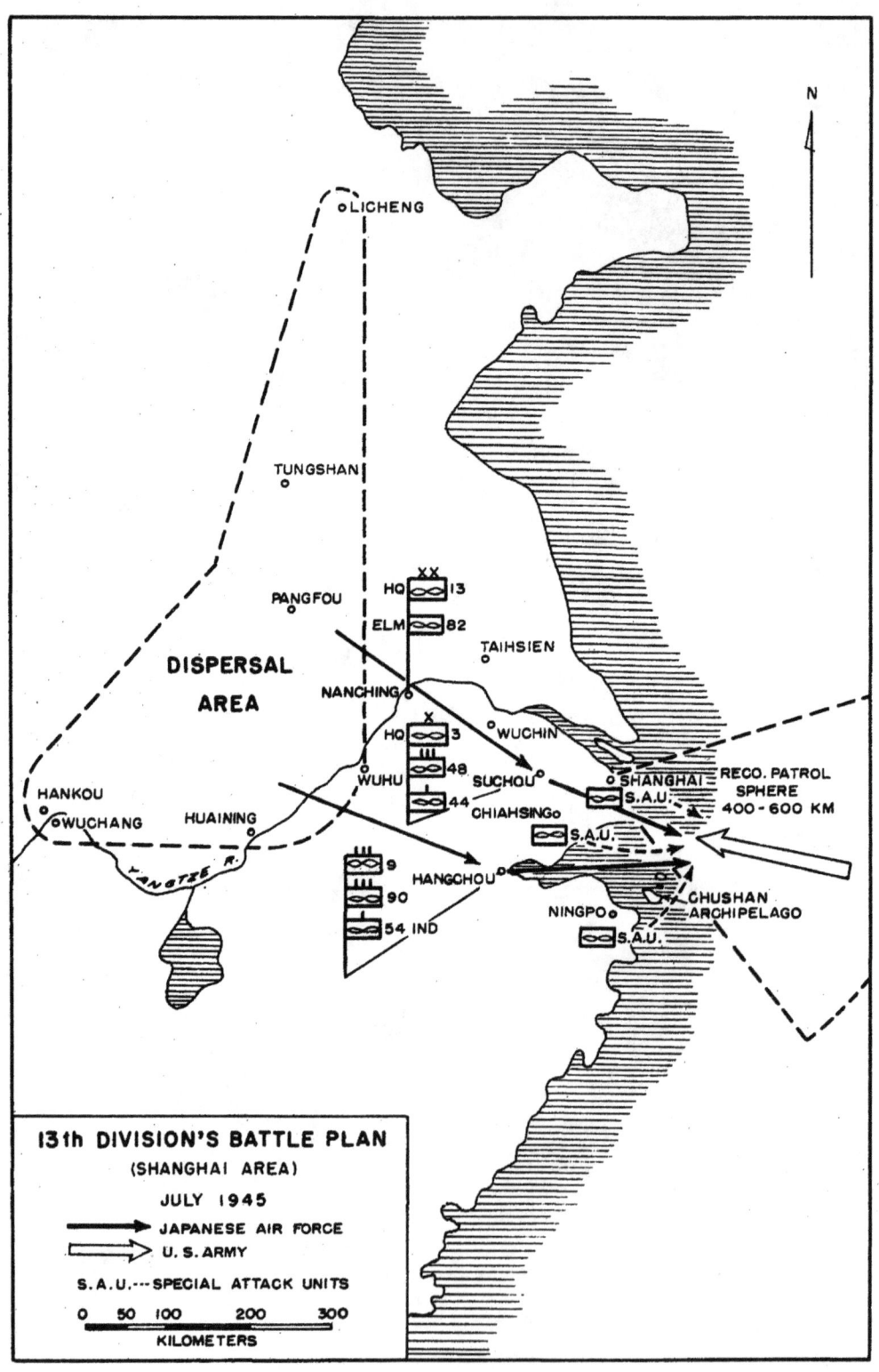

and will use its entire strength to annihilate enemy transports on the water.

Outline of Operational Command:

When an enemy attack on the triangular zone is anticipated, in order to minimize losses, air units will be withdrawn to the areas designated on Map 8.

Part of a Special Attack Unit (Type 99 twin-engine light bombers equipped with 800 kg bombs) will be disposed in the vicinity of Shanghai. This unit will endeavor to secure air superiority by attacking enemy aircraft carriers whenever the opportunity presents itself.

The base of departure for the 9th and 90th Air Regiments and the 54th Independent Air Squadron will be Hangchou while that for the 48th Air Regiment and the 2d Squadron of the 44th Air Regiment will be Suchou.

Special attacks units (composed of six to twelve planes) will be stationed at Ningpo, Chiahsing and Shanghai. These units will be prepared to launch surprise attacks against the enemy at any time.

Outline of Attacks:

The military strength to be used in each attack will be determined in accordance with the situation at the time of the engagement.

In all offensive engagements the attacking planes will enter their fields of departure from their auxiliary fields at dawn or dusk. All attacks will be launched at night, dawn or dusk. The targets will be enemy transport convoys.

The principal mission of the fighter units will be to cover the departure of the special attack units. In addition, whenever the situation demands, the fighter units will accompany and protect the main special attack units.

Situation at Termination of Hostilities

General Situation:

At the termination of hostilities, in general, preparations for air operations along the coast of central China were completed, however, it was felt that the training of the units and the lines of communication were inadequate. It was estimated that operational preparations would have been accomplished by early autumn.

As the Fifth Air Army regarded south Korea as its most important area, preparations in north China had been delayed and, at the war's end, were still in the experimental stage.

Organization:

In order to familiarize the units with the operational plan against an American attack in the central China area, war games were conducted while the command organization was trained through actual maneuvers. In this way, tactics were transmitted to even the smallest unit. The Fifth Air Army in north China and the 13th Air Division in central China cooperated in preparations for operations against the United States Air Force and were about to commence air operations in north China when the war ended.

Training of Air Units:

From early 1945, the main force of the air units in China was gradually transferred to the triangular zone. There all counterattacks were suspended and the units underwent further training. As the activities of the enemy air forces based in the interior of China intensified and at the same time attacks were made by the enemy air force based on Okinawa and from aircraft carriers, the time of training was limited to dawn and dusk. Further, due to the types of planes being used, the lack of experienced personnel and poor equipment, daylight attacks on enemy transport convoys would have resulted in heavy losses so that attacks were made only at night or at dawn.

As emphasis had been placed on improved night flying methods, the air force (with the exception of the special attack units which had been transferred from Korea and Manchuria and lacked time for training) was proficient in night combat.

Chart No. 14 shows the number of types of special attack planes used and the degree of training of their personnel at the war's end.

Construction of Air Bases:

The air bases necessary for operations against enemy attacks in the central China area, with the exception of Suchou base, generally were completed prior to the termination of hostilities. In north China, however, the repair of air bases and construction of concealed fields had not been completed.

Preparations for Lines of Communication:

The most difficult problem in regard to the preparation of lines of communication was the lack of aviation fuel. At the beginning of 1945 fuel supplies stopped. An attempt was made to transport the large quantity of fuel accumulated in central and south China and the interior to the triangular zone but enemy plane attacks made transportation difficult and it was estimated that there would be barely enough fuel in the area to conduct the Sea Coast Operation. The supply of aviation fuel in other areas was meager and just prior to the termination of hostilities the fuel shortage was seriously hampering the training of units.

Experiments in regard to the manufacture of substitute fuel were conducted but the rate of production fell far short of the rate of demand for the operations. At the war's end, all units were still endeavoring to improve the situation.

Main Air Operations:

During this period, the main air forces continued to prepare for air operations along the coast of China. They continued to improve the fighting power of the air forces and restricted operational movements as much as possible in order to train the personnel without undue loss.

The fighter units were instructed not to engage the enemy except under extremely favorable circumstances and, in consequence, the enemy air force remained practically unhampered. The twin-engine light bomber regiments, however, continued their night attacks against the enemy's advance bases and lines of communication in central and north China.

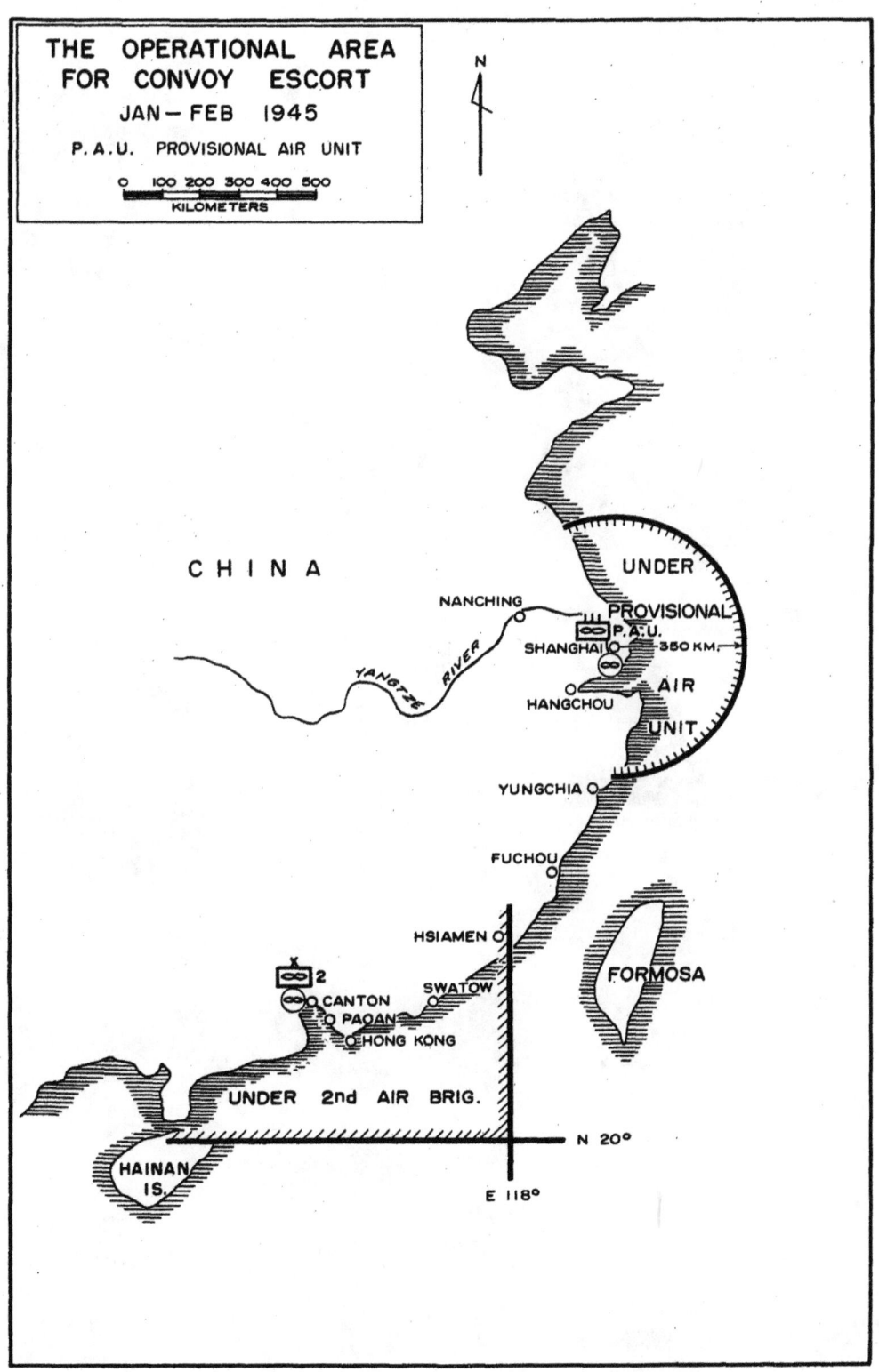

As there were no large ground operations during 1945, only one or two squadrons were required to support these operations. The main air operations during this time were:

Escort of Transport Convoys: During January and February 1945 the Army and Navy jointly undertook the transportation of fuel and other materials indispensable to the war. The China Expeditionary Army was assigned the mission of escorting these convoys, and in turn assigned areas to the 2d Air Brigade and Provisional Air Unit as shown on Map 9. The 2d Air Brigade, composed mainly of the 24th Air Regiment (Type 1 fighters) and the 41st Independent Air Squadron (Type 99 attack planes), had its main base at Canton with staging fields at Paoan, Hong Kong and Swatow, while the Provisional Air Unit, composed mainly of the 42d Independent Air Squadron (Type 99 attack planes) and the 43d Independent Air Squadron (Type 99 attack planes) operated from its base at Shanghai.

Enemy submarines lurked in the East China Sea and B-24's, based in the Philippines and the interior of China, patrolled day and night searching out and attacking convoys. The Fifth Air Army ordered the 2d Air Brigade and the Provisional Air Units to escort the transports, in cooperation with the local naval units and transport agencies.

The fighter units protected the places of shelter and convoys passing through adjacent waters while the attack and anti-submarine units patrolled the areas through which the convoys were passing and also carried out attacks against enemy submarines. As the planes were old and the personnel had no training in night flying over water, escort duty could only be carried out from dawn to dusk. The Type 99 attack planes which were used for the protection of the transport convoys were not equipped with radar and, in consequence, experienced great difficulty in locating enemy submarines. In their assigned waters, however, they were partially successful in protecting the convoys.

Air Operations During the Okinawan Campaign: As the battle for Okinawa intensified in mid-April, the 8th Air Brigade of the Fifth Air Army was ordered to participate in this operation. The units employed were:

    8th Air Brigade Headquarters

    16th Air Regiment (Type 99 twin-engine light bombers, approximately 10 planes)

    90th Air Regiment (Type 99 twin-engine light bombers, approximately 10 planes)

    Part of the 82d Air Regiment (Type 100 reconnaissance planes, two planes.)

Although the 16th and 90th Air Regiments were proficient in land night operations in China, they were inexperienced in and insufficiently equipped for sea navigation. At first, it was planned to use Shanghai, Formosa and Kyushu as take-off bases for the attack but, in view of their inexperience in sea navigation, it was finally decided that only south Kyushu would be used.

At this time, the Sixth Air Army was deployed in western Japan and was in command of air operations in the area surrounding Okinawa. By agreement with the Sixth Air Army, therefore, the 8th Air Brigade was deployed at Niitabaru and Gunzan. Gunzan was to be used as the rear air base while the Brigade was to take off from Niitabaru as frequent attacks of B-29's on the airfields in southern Kyushu made a rear staging field necessary in order to avoid losses on the ground.

The Sixth Air Army and the 8th Air Brigade, through mutual agreement, made every effort to synchronize the time of their attacks with the general attacks of the Army and Navy. In view of the limited capabilities of the Type 99 twin-engine light bombers, it was necessary to limit their objectives to destroying planes on the ground and materials stored at the airfields.

From 18 April to the end of May, the 8th Air Brigade participated in attacks against enemy air bases in Okinawa. Details of these attacks are given below:

Summary of Attacks on Enemy Air Bases on Okinawa
by Type 99 Twin-Engined Light Bombers

1. Number of planes used on each mission: About 10, Type 99 twin-engined light bombers.

2. Attack methods: Night attacks, taking advantage of the moonlight.

3. Choice of targets: Planes on the ground and dumps were the main targets of each raid.

Targets were chosen from air reconnaissance photographs.

4. Airfields used: Niitabaru Airfields were used for both take-offs and landings.

5. Method of navigation: Dead reckoning (radio silence) was used on the way to the attack to prevent enemy interference. The Southwest Islands were by-passed. Return flights were guided by the navigator.

6. Bombing methods and types of bombs used: Dive bombing from a height of 1,000 to 1,500 M.

The types of bombs used were 30 to 50 kg bombs, "TA" type bombs, and incendiary bombs.

Note: The number of personnel aboard the Type 99 twin-engined light bombers was reduced to three (pilot, engineer and a radio man); all machine guns and cannon were dismantled, and an auxiliary tank was installed to carry the maximum amount of fuel possible.

Although the actual results of the attacks could not be confirmed accurately because of antiaircraft fire and counterattacks by enemy planes, it was estimated that they were successful. Prior to the middle of May no planes were lost, but between then and the end of the month, with the completion of enemy air bases on the island, five planes were lost in night fights.

Operations Against the Russian Army

On 8 August, Russia suddenly declared war against Japan.

The China Expeditionary Army decided to use its entire air strength in China to check the enemy's advance and ordered the 13th Air Division, which had been deployed in the triangular zone in preparation for operations against the sea front, to north China. The 13th Air Division first dispatched the 90th Air Regiment (Type 99 twin-engine light bombers), the 54th Independent Air Squadron (Type 98 direct cooperation planes) and part of the 81st Air Regiment (Type 100 reconnaissance planes) to north China and planned later to deploy its entire strength in that area.

By the evening of 14 August the first units were deployed on Peiping airfields and the same evening air reconnaissance planes reported an enemy mechanized force moving in the area north of Changpei. Early the following morning, the main force of the 90th Air Regiment (20 bombers) attacked this enemy force. Then, on receipt of an Imperial edict promulgating the termination of hostilities, all action was suspended.

The war ended before the main force of the Air Division had advanced to north China.

INDEX

Air Armies
  General: 192
  1st: 168n
  2d: 113n
  5th: 143-45, 148-52, 155, 157-62, 168, 173, 176-77, 183-84, 190-93, 202, 207, 208
  6th: 209

Air Battalions
  1st: 16, 36
  2d: 16, 37
  3d: 16, 30, 36
  5th: 16, 30, 36-37
  6th: 16, 36
  7th: 36
  8th: 16, 30, 37
  9th: 16, 36
  10th: 20n, 22
  11th: 20n
  12th: 19, 20n
  15th: 19, 20n
  16th: 19, 20n

Air Brigades
  1st: 15, 23-25, 52-56, 59-60, 63, 71, 74, 77-78, 80, 82, 87, 89, 93-95, 97-98, 103, 106-11, 119, 123, 124, 126, 134-35, 143, 152, 159, 160, 173, 176
  2d: 150, 153, 155, 161, 173, 176-77, 191, 207
  3d: 28, 30, 37, 41-42, 44, 46-47, 52-56, 59-60, 63, 74, 76-78, 80, 83, 87-89, 95-98, 192, 195
  4th: 23-24, 26, 37, 40, 41, 53-55, 55n, 56, 63, 76, 78, 95, 96
  7th: 59, 60, 63, 74
  8th: 128-29, 133-34, 136, 173, 178, 184, 208-09
  16th: 153
  Composite: 19
  Fujita: 45
  Giga: 38-40
  Provisional: 19-20, 22, 25
  Terakura: 44-45, 45n
  Training 105th: 144

Air Divisions
  2d: 150n
  3d: 111, 113, 119-23, 125, 127, 129, 131-32, 134, 136-37, 139, 143
  5th: 128
  8th: 168n
  13th: 191-95, 202, 211

Air Group: 48-49, 52-54, 56, 59, 60-63, 71, 74-75, 77, 85, 93-94

Air Groups
  1st: 97
  2d: 20
  3d: 77-78, 81, 85, 87-88, 92, 95-96, 103, 111
  5th: 106, 106n
  Provisional: 15-16, 19-20, 22-23, 25, 27, 30, 36-38, 40, 44, 45n, 46, 49

Air Regiments
  6th: 150, 152-53, 155, 169, 173, 176, 178
  8th: 95-96
  9th: 144, 149-50, 155, 169, 193, 201
  10th: 45, 45n, 77-78
  11th: 78, 89
  12th: 58-60, 63, 69, 73-74, 98, 98n
  14th: 95-96
  15th: 58-60, 74, 89, 97
  16th: 112, 119, 121-23, 135, 143, 150, 155, 161, 169, 183, 208
  22d: 168, 168n

23d: 119
24th: 110, 112, 207
25th: 119, 121-24, 126, 133-35, 143, 149-50, 152, 155, 160, 169
27th: 57n, 60, 63, 74, 77
29th: 168, 168n
31st: 55, 55n, 63, 83, 89
32d: 96-97
33d: 113, 119, 121-24, 126, 133-36
44th: 80, 95, 97-98, 103, 106, 110, 112, 119-20, 124, 143, 150, 152-53, 155, 169, 173, 176, 178, 186, 193, 201
45th: 60, 76-77, 104, 104n
48th: 150, 152, 155, 169, 193, 201
54th: 104, 110, 112
58th: 128-29, 133-34
59th: 63, 75, 78, 80-81, 93-95
60th: 55, 60, 69, 73, 77-78, 81-82, 87-89, 92, 94-95, 98, 128-29, 134, 168, 168n
62d: 109, 111
64th: 55, 57n, 60, 63, 77, 83, 89
65th: 111-13
75th: 60, 76, 80, 95-96, 98
77th: 60, 76-77
81st: 193, 211
82d: 169, 208
83d: 96-97
85th: 128-29, 135-36, 143, 153, 155, 161, 169
90th: 57n, 60, 74, 77, 87, 93, 95, 97-98, 109-10, 112, 119, 121-22, 126, 135, 143, 150, 153, 155, 161, 169, 183, 193, 201, 208, 211
98th: 55, 60, 69, 73, 77, 98, 98n

Air Squadrons
  3d Ind: 16, 36
  4th Ind: 16, 37
  6th Ind: 16, 37
  9th Ind: 16, 36
  10th Ind: 37, 60, 77, 81, 92, 95, 97, 104, 110, 112
  11th Ind: 37
  15th Ind: 37
  16th Ind: 60, 77, 81, 92, 98
  17th Ind: 60, 76, 80, 92, 98
  18th Ind: 52, 60, 70, 76, 94, 103, 110-11, 119, 134, 144, 153, 155, 162
  41st Ind: 207
  42d Ind: 207
  43d Ind: 207
  54th Ind: 144, 150, 152, 155, 169, 173, 176, 178, 186, 193, 201, 211
  55th Ind: 113, 119, 124, 135, 144, 153, 157, 162
  66th Ind: 103, 103n
  82d Ind: 80
  83d Ind: 103, 110, 112, 124
  84th Ind: 80
  85th Ind: 119
  87th Ind: 103, 103n

Air Units
  Aoki: 36
  21st Ind: 77, 80, 83, 89
  29th Ind: 112
  206th Ind: 110, 112, 120, 135
  209th Ind: 110
  Nakahira: 38-39
  North China Area Army: 57, 57n, 58, 60
  Provisional: 22, 152, 160, 207
  Seto: 119
  Sudo: 57, 57n
  Training Fifth: 135
  Yamase: 38-39, 57
  Direct Cooperation
    1st: 63
    8th: 104, 110, 120
Aleutians: 108
Ani: 37, 58n, 59, 62-63, 71, 73, 81, 92, 97-98, 122

Ankang: 62, 146, 187-88
Anyang: 25, 37-38, 41, 45, 57-58, 58n, 62, 112, 143, 161
Area Armies
  Central China: 30, 41, 46
  North China: 23, 30, 38-39, 44, 46, 52, 57-58, 58n, 59-60, 62-63, 74-75, 87, 96-97, 112, 120, 144
  South China: 93, 95
Armies
  Central China Expeditionary: 44, 47, 49, 52-53, 60, 62, 74-75
  China Expeditionary: 80-81, 87, 96-97, 103n, 106-07, 111, 113-14, 117-18, 121, 129, 134-35, 138, 144, 168, 185, 187, 190, 192, 207, 211
  Kwantung: 17n, 19-22, 25, 45n, 58-59, 96-97
  Mongolia Garrison: 58-59
  North China Garrison: 16, 19-21
  Shanghai Expeditionary: 23, 27-28, 30-31, 41
  Southern: 118, 128-29, 136-37
  First: 23-24, 38, 45-46, 57-59, 97
  Second: 23-25, 27, 38-39, 44-46, 46n, 52-56, 59
  Fifth: 37
  Tenth: 30-31, 42
  Eleventh: 52-56, 60, 63, 87, 106, 109, 112, 120, 144-45, 147, 151, 153, 159, 160, 164-65, 173, 178
  Twelfth: 186
  Thirteenth: 87, 95-96, 109, 112, 120
  Twentieth: 186
  Twenty-first: 55, 55n, 56, 58, 58n, 63
  Twenty-third: 104, 120, 144, 153, 161, 165, 173, 177, 179, 195

Bay
  Hangchou: 30
Brigades
  Ind Mixed
    5th: 57-58
    11th: 20
  Mixed
    2d: 20
Burma: 128, 138
Canton: 63, 69, 103, 110-11, 113, 121, 125, 131-32, 134-35, 137, 143, 161, 173, 176, 179, 190-91, 207
Cavalry Group: 57-58
Central Authorities: 15, 16
Chahar Expeditionary Group: 22
Changan: 26, 40, 45, 45n, 48, 59, 62, 82, 146, 187-88
Changhsing: 31
Changpei: 211
Changsha: 56, 106, 151, 158, 160
Changtien: 120
Chanyi: 127, 132, 189
Chaoan: 32
Chaotung: 189
Chenghsien: 149, 186
Chengkung: 189
Chengte: 20-21
Chengtu: 66, 73, 82-83, 91-93, 127, 146-47, 168, 180-81, 183, 186, 189
Chiahsien: 35, 82
Chiahsing: 201
Chian: 56, 62, 85, 131, 136
Chiang
  Chientang: 41, 85
  Han: 69
  Hsi: 165
  Hsiang: 151, 185
Chiang Kai-shek: 72
Chiangtu: 38
Chienchuntai: 22
Chienou: 107, 124, 131-33
Chihcheng: 21
Chihkiang: 63, 66, 85, 127, 132, 147, 162, 164, 173, 176, 178-79, 185, 188

China Incident: 15, 16, 22, 28
Chinese Division
   143d: 19
Chinghuayuan: 19
Chingtao: 53
Chingyuan: 24
Chinhsien: 20
Chinhua: 85
Chokai: 90
Chouchiakou: 26, 35, 44
Chuhsien: 85, 107-10
Chujung: 27-28
Chungking: 56, 62-63, 66, 71-72, 83, 87, 91-93, 97, 112, 127, 130-31, 133, 138, 146-47, 164, 186
Chushan Archipelago: 190, 195
Detachments
   Hata: 42, 49
   Sakamoto: 45
   Sakata: 20
   Sato: 43
   Seya: 45
   Shigeto: 28
   Ushijima: 22
Divisions
   3d: 42-43, 47-48
   5th: 20-21, 25, 57, 95
   6th: 42, 47, 49, 52
   9th: 48
   10th: 23
   13th: 42, 47-48
   14th: 39, 46, 46n
   16th: 46
   18th: 42, 63
   20th: 22, 25, 39
   21st: 58, 97
   22d: 95
   35th: 97
   38th: 105-06, 106n
   101st: 43
   104th: 63
   106th: 55
   108th: 39
   109th: 39
   110th: 57, 59
   114th: 57, 58
East China Sea: 187, 207
Eijiro Ebashi, Maj Gen: 63
Einosuke Sudo, Col: 57n
Enshih: 62, 140, 146, 150, 162, 187-88
Erhtaokou: 54-55
Fenyang: 25
Fleet
   3d: 80
Formosa: 27, 37, 78, 97, 134-35, 181-82, 208
French Indo-China: 92-94, 130-31, 133-34, 148
Fuchou: 95, 123
Fushih: 59, 82
Great Canal: 39
Gunzan: 209
Haikoushih: 119, 128
Hangchou: 27, 38, 41-43, 47, 52-53, 55, 95-96, 110-12, 191, 193, 195, 201
Hankou: 31, 35, 49, 52-54, 56, 59-60, 63, 69, 71, 87, 92, 98, 110, 119, 129, 135, 143-44, 152, 158, 161, 179-80, 190-93
Hanoi: 134
Hantan: 38
Hanyang: 69
Heito: 136
Hengshan: 56
Hengyang: 56, 62, 85, 107, 109, 113, 121, 124-27, 132, 147, 151, 158-62, 164-65, 168, 173, 176-78, 186
Hisao Hozoji, Maj Gen: 59
Ho
   Huai: 42, 48, 53
   Huang: 24, 27, 29, 46, 145, 149
   New Huang: 57
   Sha: 24
   Shih: 55
   Suchou: 30
   Tayun: 39n
Hofei: 35, 52, 54

Hohsien: 24, 44
Hong Kong: 103-06, 132, 207
Hsiangtan: 158, 160
Hsiangyang: 35, 40
Hsiaochihkou: 52-54, 148, 152
Hsiaochou: 134
Hsienhsien: 24
Hsincheng: 177
Hsingtai: 24
Hsinhsiang: 37, 58, 96-97, 112, 149-50
Hsinkouchen: 25
Hsinshih: 158
Hsinyang: 35, 41, 44, 48, 55, 111
Hsuchang: 186
Huailai: 21
Huaining: 52-53, 55, 148
Huaiyuan: 48
Huangchuan: 54-55
Huanghoyai: 27
Huangmei: 53
Hukou: 52
Ichang: 87
Ichuan: 82
Imperial General Headquarters: 37, 49, 60-61, 74, 77-78, 80-81, 88, 93, 96-97, 107-09, 111, 113, 117-18, 128, 135, 143, 168, 185, 190
Islands
  Chungmingtao: 43
  Hainan: 125, 128
  Midway: 108
  Morell: 108
  Saipan: 181
  Saishu To: 27
  Southwest: 210
  Stonecutter: 105
Jochi: 55
Juichang: 55
Kagi: 134-36
Kaifeng: 26, 149
Kailuan (coal mine): 125
Kaitak: 105, 128
Kamijo, Col: 20

Kamikawamaru: 90
Kanhsien: 85, 136-37, 161-62, 165, 168, 176-79, 186
Kaoi: 25
Kingmen: 98, 113
Korea: 192, 192n, 193, 202
Kowloon Peninsula: 105
Kuangchi: 55
Kuangte: 28, 31, 42
Kungta: 28
Kunming (Yunnan): 83, 136, 147, 186, 189
Kweilin: 66, 105, 107, 109, 113, 120-23, 125-27, 130-32, 134, 136-38, 140, 143, 145, 147, 150, 153, 158, 161-62, 164-65, 168, 172-73, 176-79
Kweiyang: 56, 83, 147, 188
Kyushu: 208-09
Laifengyi: 189
Lanchow: 26, 35, 59, 62, 72-73, 82-83, 128
Lanfeng: 45-46, 48
Laohokou: 122, 146, 162, 178, 185, 187
Laohwangping: 188
Lianghsiang: 22
Liangshan: 56, 62, 66, 83, 92, 123, 126-37, 140, 146, 150, 162, 178, 187-88
Licheng: 27, 37, 39, 58, 110, 112, 180, 193
Lincheng: 37, 53
Linfen: 37, 39-40, 58n
Lingling: 113, 122-27, 132, 139, 173, 177-78
Lishui: 107-09, 124
Liuchowhsien: 62, 66, 113, 122-23, 143, 147, 153, 161-62, 164-65, 168, 173, 176-79
Lochuan: 82
Loshan: 55
Loyang: 26, 35, 40, 82
Luhsien: 92
Luichow Peninsula: 119
Lupouchiao Incident: 19, 21

Luliang: 189
Lungchou: 83
Lunghuachen: 31
Lushih: 122
Machang: 23
Manchuria: 15-16, 19, 22, 77, 97, 110n-11n, 113, 113n, 128, 144, 147, 168, 180-84, 192n, 193, 203
Masao Yamase, Col: 38, 40, 57n
Mengcheng: 48
Mengtzu: 83, 125, 189
Moji: 181
Moritaka Nakazono, Lt Gen: 134
Mountains
  Lushan: 55
  Tapiehshan: 56
Nanchang: 27, 35, 56, 110, 112, 120
Nancheng: 35, 62, 82, 121, 146, 188
Nanching: 27, 28, 31, 37, 41-44, 47, 52-53, 55, 85, 110, 119, 129, 135, 143-44, 150, 179-80, 186, 191-93
Nanchwan: 92
Nanhsiangchen: 28
Nanhsiung: 54, 133, 136-37, 177
Nanning: 125, 136, 147, 188
Nanpingchi: 48
Nantung: 43
Nanyang: 56, 144, 146
Nanyuan: 19, 21, 22-23, 26, 45, 53, 59, 81, 87
Nanyuehshih: 56
Navy
  Air Divisions
    1st: 76
    3d: 76
    12th: 89, 93
    13th: 89, 93
    14th: 76, 90, 93
    15th: 90, 93
  Air Units
    Chingtao: 77-78, 89
    Hainan Island Base: 90
    Kanoya: 93
    River Base Flying: 89
    Takao: 76, 93
  Combined Air Force
    1st: 26, 76, 82
  Combined Air Units (Group)
    2d: 76, 80, 82, 89, 93
    3d: 80, 90, 93
Neichiu: 25
Niitabaru: 209, 210
Ningpo: 195, 201
Ningsia: 59
Nomonhan Incident: 77
Okinawa: 185-86, 190, 192, 194, 203, 208-09
Operation
  Canton: 37, 56, 58n
  Chahar: 20
  Changte: 139
  Chekiang-Kiangsi: 107, 109
  Chihkiang: 186
  Chohsien-Chingyuan: 24
  Chungyuan: 96-97
  Eastern Chekiang: 95-96
  Hong Kong: 103, 103n, 104, 104n
  Hopeh: 38, 40
  Hunan-Kwangsi: 144, 146, 151-53, 158, 164, 185
  Ichang: 87
  Ichi-Go: 140n, 143, 145, 147, 157, 158-59, 162, 164-65, 168, 172, 180, 182
  Laohokou: 186
  Luichow Peninsula: 119
  Nanching: 30, 35
  Nanning: 83
  No. 102: 97
  Peiping-Hankou: 144-45, 149, 153, 162
  2d Changsha: 106, 106n
  Shanghai: 31
  Suichuan-Kanhsien: 185
  Tago: 82
  Tungshan: 35, 46n, 47-49, 57
  Wu-Han: 48-49, 53, 57, 69-70

Yangchu: 25-26
Outer Great Wall: 21
Pailochi: 152, 158-60, 165, 173, 176-77
Paise: 188
Paishachou: 158
Paishihyi: 189
Paiyangkou: 21
Pangfou: 38, 47-48, 53
Paoan: 207
Paochi: 82, 132, 146
Paotou: 62-63
Patung: 133, 136
Peiping: 19, 40, 57, 58n, 110, 112, 180, 211
Pengtse: 52-53, 55
Pingliang: 82
Pishan: 92
Poshan: 189
Provinces
  Anhwei: 42
  Chahar: 17n, 20, 22
  Chekiang: 42, 95, 107-09, 112
  Fukien: 62, 90, 112, 123-24, 146
  Honan: 61-62, 81, 90, 150
  Hopeh: 20, 23
  Hunan: 111-12, 180
  Kansu: 61-62, 90
  Kiangsi: 109, 112
  Kwangsi: 62, 90, 111-12, 180
  Kwangtung: 62, 90
  Ninghsia: 62
  Shansi: 38, 45, 58, 73
  Shantung: 57, 61, 90, 120
  Shensi: 61-62, 81, 90, 150
  Suiyuan: 62
  Szechwan: 71, 81, 91, 117-18, 130, 133, 145-47
  Yunnan: 62, 90, 117, 126-28, 130-34, 136-38, 146-47
Puchi: 120, 160
Putien: 124
Rivers
  Huangpu: 27
  Yangtze: 31, 49, 95, 98, 106, 120, 131, 139, 146-48, 151-52, 176, 179, 185-86, 194

Railways
  Canton-Hankou: 32, 56, 143, 147, 165, 168, 176
  Canton-Kowloon: 32, 147
  Chekiang-Kiangsi: 41-42, 95
  Hunan-Kwangsi: 143
  Indo China-Yunnan: 91
  Lunghai: 21, 26, 38, 41, 44-46, 58, 192
  Peiping-Hankou: 25, 27, 38, 44-45, 58-59, 143, 149, 182-83
  Tatung-Puchow: 39
  Tienching-Pukou: 41-42, 44-45, 47, 179-80, 182-83
Rokuro Imanishi, Maj Gen: 134
Ryuichi Torida, Col: 40
Saburo Ando, Maj Gen: 20
Saigon: 103, 134
Sanchoushan Mountain Range: 43
Santouping: 133
Sanya: 125, 128
Seoul: 192
Shangchin: 40, 44, 48, 53, 58n
Shanghai: 21, 23, 27-28, 85, 111, 135, 180, 190-91, 193, 195, 201, 207
Shanghuayuan: 21
Shangjao: 85
Shaochow: 54
Shaoyang: 186
Shehsien: 35
Shihchiachuang: 24, 25, 37, 58n
Shozo Terakura, Maj Gen: 45, 71
Singapore: 111
Suchien: 44
Suchou: 195, 203
Suichuan: 136-37, 150-51, 161, 165, 168, 176, 178-79, 186
Suining: 92, 189
Swatow: 32, 207
Tachangchen: 28, 95-96, 129, 143
Tadatsugu Chiga, Maj Gen: 28
Taierhchuang: 44
Taihsien: 120, 193
Takeo Aoki, Capt: 36n
Taku: 53
Takuma Shimoyama, Lt Gen: 134
Tancheng: 44

Tanchuhsu: 147, 173, 178
Tatung: 20-21, 57
Tawenkou: 39
Tean: 55
Tehsien: 27
Tetsuji Giga, Maj Gen: 38, 45
Tienchen: 21
Tienchiachen: 55
Tienching: 15, 19, 23, 25, 57, 58n
Tolun: 20-21
Tomo Fujita, Maj Gen: 40, 63
Tourane: 134
Tsanghsien: 24
Tsingchen: 188
Tuhshan: 188
Tungliang: 92
Tungshan: 40-41, 43-44, 46, 48, 53, 57-58, 143, 161
Tungtai: 38
Tzeliutsing: 92, 97
Tzuyang: 45
Wanchuan: 19-21
Wangpin: 28, 31, 52-53
Wanhsien: 123, 133

Wuchang: 53, 59, 69, 98, 135, 158, 161, 173, 179, 190
Wuchin: 31, 193
Wuchou: 133, 173
Wu-Han: 59, 69, 87, 112, 119, 126, 130, 151, 158, 165, 173, 177
Wuhu: 31, 38, 43, 47-48, 148
Wuyuan: 59
Yangchieh: 189
Yangchu: 22, 25-27, 37-38, 57, 58n, 112, 144
Yangkao: 22, 25
Yangmingpao: 25
Yaotienkung: 24
Yawata: 181
Yingtanchen: 85
Yoshitoshi Tokugawa, Lt Gen, Baron: 15, 36
Yoyang: 59, 69
Yuanshih: 25
Yuling: 125
Yungchia: 195
Yunnanyi: 189
Yushan: 35, 56, 85, 107-09, 144

www.ingramcontent.com/pod-product-compliance
Lightning Source LLC
Chambersburg PA
CBHW080440170426
43195CB00017B/2834